The William J. Burns International Detective Agency, Inc. is pleased to present to you a complimentary first edition of the biography of William J. Burns.

The agency and members of the Burns family are grateful to Prentice-Hall for publishing this faithful account of the exploits of our founder. The ingenuity and thoroughness of the original William J. Burns, we believe, characterizes the work we are doing in the security field today.

We trust the reading is enjoyable and rewarding.

Sincerely,

RAYMOND J. BURNS
W. SHERMAN BURNS
WILLIAM J. BURNS
D. BRUCE BURNS

INCREDIBLE
DETECTIVE

The Biography of William J. Burns

GENE CAESAR

Prentice-Hall, Inc., Englewood Cliffs, N.J.

*This book
is for
Craig Arthur Caesar
born October 28
1961.*

INCREDIBLE DETECTIVE
The Biography of William J. Burns
by Gene Caesar

©1968 by Gene Caesar

Library of Congress Catalog Card Number: 68-12816

Printed in the United States of America

T

Prentice-Hall International, Inc., London
Prentice-Hall of Australia, Pty. Ltd., Sydney
Prentice-Hall of Canada, Ltd., Toronto
Prentice-Hall of India Private Ltd., New Delhi
Prentice-Hall of Japan, Inc., Tokyo

CONTENTS

A Note on Sources

Any narrative of this type is something of a collective effort, not only assisted but to a large extent rendered possible by the efforts of individuals too numerous to name. However, this book's debt to Mrs. Kathleen King and Mrs. Florence Borough must certainly be acknowledged, and to Raymond and W. Sherman Burns of the William J. Burns International Detective Agency. These four surviving children of this biography's subject have never failed to respond promptly and patiently to endless requests for information over a period of several years; yet on no occasion did any of them attempt to influence the historical judgments that had to be made.

Further acknowledgment should go to Chief James J. Rowley of the United States Secret Service; to James Babcock, Chief of the Burton Historical Collection at the Detroit Public Library, and to Mrs. Lenore Harrington of the Missouri Historical Society.

This book contains a great deal of dialogue, all of which is "source" dialogue, although extensively abridged in many instances. Some of these conversations were recalled in courtroom testimony; others were included in the accounts of newsmen and letter writers present at various events. But the great bulk of the dialogue used in this narrative, and therefore the great weight of its authenticity, rests directly with William

J. Burns, who almost invariably included dramatized conversations in his interviews with reporters and magazine writers.

An attempt has been made here to compensate the great detective's recollections in allowance for his inclination to make a good story improve with age. His later versions of several cases, although not really contradicting his contemporary or courtroom accounts, do contain added anecdotes — invariably amusing and frequently only indirectly connected. Such additions are not included here (but may be enjoyed by anyone who wishes to browse in the bibliography that follows). In certain early cases, where neither courtroom records nor detailed news accounts are available for a cross-check, similar anecdotes have been deleted from the versions Burns gave in his later years of celebrity.

This narrative has further attempted, in its judgment of sources, to make the best possible estimate of the capabilities of the chroniclers. The writings about Burns by Lincoln Steffens, for example, are probably colored only by Steffens' delight in finding evidence to sustain a belief that the government and the large corporations of his era were inherently corrupt. The writings of Harvey J. O'Higgins, on the other hand, are saturated with hero-worship of Burns, with obvious awe at the very fact that the great detective would grant him an interview.

Any attempt to include a complete bibliography of the books consulted in the researching of this story would run to a great many pages and would be of no use to either the casual student or the professional historian working in related subject matter, since few books have been more than the most minor type of source on this subject. The standard local histories, such as those of the City of Columbus, Ohio, or Ripley County, Indiana, have been helpful. And such recent works as Lately Thomas' *A Debonair Scoundrel,* Hugh Bailie's *High Tension,* or Harry Golden's *A Little Girl is Dead* have been of substantial assistance, in the areas where they touch upon Burns' career.

Yet by way of contrast, the very books that might reasonably have been expected to make an even greater contribution to a Burns biography have been of no value in this respect.

In *The United States Secret Service,* by Walter Bowen and Harry Neal, the story of the Philadelphia-Lancaster counterfeiting case is actually told with no mention of the name of the operative to whom Secret Service Chief John Wilkie gave full credit for solving the case.

This strange omission cannot be shrugged off to the fact that Secret Service records from that period were kept for only a short length of time; both newspaper sources and numerous official documents were readily available to the authors. Furthermore, Burns was patently slighted on many other occasions in this puzzling book and even subjected to vague, undocumented insinuations in some portions.

There is of course a resentment, in any government service, of the man who forsakes a secure but plodding promotion schedule and achieves striking success in related private work. There was, in the early 1920's, serious antagonism between the Secret Service and the F.B.I. The work of Bowen and Neal, apparently researched chiefly from the recollections of old-timers, reflects, intentionally or otherwise, both this antagonism and this resentment.

Although Don Whitehead's *The F.B.I. Story* and Fred Cook's *The F.B.I. Nobody Knows* represent two diametrically opposed viewpoints in most respects, both paint equally false pictures of William J. Burns. Cook perhaps failed to do his homework; he knew little of Burns' career prior to 1921 and very probably did not consider such knowledge germane to his purpose.

Whitehead, however, cannot be let off so lightly.

Whenever *The F.B.I. Story* touched upon Burns' successes— in the Western lands-frauds cases, for example—the author avoided mentioning the great detective's name, identifying him only as a former Secret Service operative. Yet Whitehead then names Burns in relating the thoroughly discredited political charges made by the Taft wing of the Republican Party arising from the same cases.

Whitehead further blames Burns for all that was wrong with the early F.B.I. and credits Burns' young assistant J. Edgar Hoover with all that the F.B.I. accomplished during the period. The author's obvious hero worship may be well-placed. But Mr. Hoover can stand on his own record as director of the F.B.I. No chronicler need resort to such deception to enhance his history by slighting his predecessor.

One more book must be mentioned, although not necessarily in criticism, since it makes no pretense of being history. In *Final Verdict,* Adela Rogers St. John speaks of "the lies I tell here for my father," and again, "I have told lies to protect us, but they do not matter." With all due allowance for the author's fierce devotion to her father and her resulting determination to discredit his antagonists, this reasoning must be challenged. William J. Burns has surviving daughters as well.

Newspaper sources have played a major part in the compilation of this biography. Here again, any detailed listing of news items would be useless to the general reader and a repetition of the obvious for the serious student. In general, *The New York Times,* published with an avowed aim of being the paper of record fifty years hence, has served that purpose admirably here, and has been used as a running index throughout, from the first accounts of the Ohio tally-sheets fraud in 1885 to Burns' death in 1932. In various individual cases, the newspapers of Columbus, St. Louis, Philadelphia, San Francisco, Los Angeles and Atlanta have served as prime sources, from the first pertinent news stories through the accounts of trials and appeals.

For any reader wishing to probe further into the subject, the best bibliography that can be offered lies in the many periodical articles written about the great detective, the bulk of which are available at most major libraries. There is a great deal of praise in these articles, but there is no lack of criticism, some of it severe. In many cases, the political viewpoint of the publication must be considered. But as a whole, this listing will provide an excellent insight into the era, adventures, and place in history of William J. Burns.

Burns, William J.,

"Disappearance of Edna Kent," *Woman's Home Companion,* December, 1915.

"Heir to the Willis Fortune," *Woman's Home Companion,* March & April, 1916.

"Hotel and Bank Crooks," *Saturday Evening Post*, June 6, 1925.

"How Safe is Your Home?", *Popular Mechanics,* May, 1932.

"How Women Are Robbed," *Ladies Home Journal,* October, 1914.

"Immigration Work of the Bureau of Investigation," *Congressional Digest,* July, 1923.

"Port of Missing Men," *Popular Mechanics,* June, 1932.

"Trail of the Bank Swindler," *Saturday Evening Post*, June 13, 1925.

"Woman in the Case," *Woman's Home Companion,* October, 1915.

Editorial,

"The American Cheka," *Freeman,* February 28, 1923.

"American Dynamiters," *London Spectator,* January 6, 1912.

"Detective Burns and his Psychological Method," *Current Literature,* June, 1911.

"History of William J. Burns," *The Nation,* November 23, 1927.

"Star of the Secret Service," *Overland Monthly,* January, 1908.

"William J. Burns," *McClure's,* February, 1911.

Gatlin, Dana.

"How Abe Ruef Confessed," *McClure's,* February, 1911.

"The Monroe-Head Counterfeit," *McClure's,* March, 1911.

"Tracking Anonymous Letter Writers," *McClure's*, April, 1911.

"Ulrich, A Soldier of Fortune," *McClure's*, May. 1911.

Hynd, Alan.

"America's Front-Page Detective," *True*, March, 1951.

"The Case of the Dynamite Murders," *True*, May, 1946.

"Trackdown of the Dynamiters," *True,* February, 1962.

O'Higgins, Harvey J.,

"The Amateur Detective," *McClure's*, November, 1911.

"The Arson Mysteries," *McClure's*, January, 1912.

"A Case of Corruption," *McClure's*, August, 1912.

"The Dynamiters," *McClure's*, August 1911.

"Finessing," *McClure's*, June 1912.

"Gompers Speaks Out for Labor," *McClure's*, January, 1912.

"How Burns Caught the Dynamiters," *McClure's*, January, 1912.

"The Insurance Salesman," *McClure's*, October, 1911.

"On the Trail of the Men Higher Up," *McClure's*, February, 1912.

"A Promoter of Counterfeits," *McClure's,* September, 1911.

"Some Burns Plants," *McClure's*, March 1912.

Reeves, Arthur B.,

"The Mystery of the Double Eagles," *McClure's*, October, 1912.

Steffens, Lincoln,

"The Making of a Fighter," *American,* August, 1907.

"A Ring-Robbed Railroad," *Everybody's Magazine*, April, 1911.

"The Taming of the West," *American*, May, June, July, August, September, October, 1907.

PART ONE

The Making of a Supersleuth

The year was 1899. The Boer War had just begun in South Africa. And in Washington, D.C., a most unnerving note turned up in the morning mail of Lord Julian Pauncefote, the British ambassador to the United States. Bearing a Detroit, Michigan, postmark but neither name nor return address, the printed message was brief and explicit: Unless Great Britain gave up its aggression against the Transvaal and the Orange Free State immediately, the anonymous note writer was coming to Washington to put a bullet through Lord Pauncefote's head.

The ambassador took the message directly to Secretary of State John Hay, who assured him that it was most likely a crank letter making an empty threat. "We'll have the Secret Service check it out immediately," Hay promised. "I'll personally ask Chief John Wilkie to assign one of his best men."

"One of his best men" Flustered and frightened, the lord's courtliness left him for the moment. "What can one man do? What could a dozen men do, or your entire Secret Service? This could have been sent by anyone living in Detroit. Or simply posted there by someone living somewhere else, anywhere else. Even if you had men enough to examine and compare the handwriting of an entire city, it wouldn't help. This is printing. Show me one thing about this note

13

that could possibly lead to the man who is threatening my life"

Ambassador Pauncefote found it difficult to concentrate on diplomacy that day and even more difficult to sleep through the night that followed. He called on the Secretary of State again in the morning, but he found little comfort in Hay's assurance that the Secret Service was already hard at work on the matter.

"Wilkie has called an operative in from the New York district office," John Hay said, soothingly. "The man who broke that big counterfeiting case in Pennsylvania."

"That," Lord Julian observed dryly, "took more than a year."

The British diplomat had another uneasy day to endure and another restless night. But then, to his amazement, the Secretary of State brought him the relieving news that the threatening letter writer was in custody.

"How?" the ambassador gasped. "How could he possibly have been found in just two days? There wasn't a thing in that note to identify him."

Hay shrugged his shoulders. The Secret Service's methods were indeed secret. All he knew was that the threat-maker had turned out to be an old man and obviously harmless — merely a former resident of the Transvaal who had let his strong feelings about the war get the better of him. Considering this, Hay wondered, did Lord Julian wish to press charges? Or would another note, one of apology, settle the matter?

Ambassador Pauncefote was perfectly willing to accept the apology. But he was most unwilling to let the infuriating question of how the letter had been traced go unanswered. He demanded to see Chief John Wilkie. Then, when Wilkie remained smilingly evasive, the ambassador insisted that the operative who had solved the seemingly insoluble puzzle be sent to him.

Lord Julian was startled when a short, stocky fellow with

flame-red hair and a matching mustache entered his office the next morning and introduced himself as William J. Burns. Florid in speech as well as complexion, the man was far more suggestive of a successful salesman or even a theatrical personality than a highly skilled detective. Furthermore, although he was actually 38, he looked much younger — too young to enjoy such a reputation.

"The printing on this note was a dead giveaway," Burns explained.

"But it's such a simple style of printing," the ambassador protested. "It's crude, in fact. The 'T's are only half-crossed, and it's all in capital letters. There are no flourishes of any sort."

"That's just it," Burns said. "Everything is too simple. There isn't the slightest wasted movement of the pen anywhere. Notice how each letter begins at the bottom left? How the 'A' is made with two strokes instead of three? How the 'B' was done without lifting the pen from the paper?" He demonstrated. "This is obviously the work of a man who has learned to print as rapidly as possible. Now why does a man learn this? For what sort of job?" He paused purposefully.

"A telegrapher, perhaps?" Ambassador Pauncefote finally asked.

"Right." Burns nodded approvingly, like an encouraging schoolteacher prodding a promising pupil. "It's just common sense." Then he went on to explain that he'd come to this conclusion immediately upon examining the note, that he'd caught the next train for Detroit and presented first his credentials and then the anonymous letter to the chief operator at one of the two telegraph stations there.

"I didn't ask him if he recognized the printing, of course."

"Of course," Lord Julian echoed, wondering why.

"That would have been practically inviting him to say no. I told him, 'This was written by one of your telegraphers,

15

and I want to know which one.' That made him study the note a while and do some hard thinking about it."

If the ambassador had expected a highly regarded government investigator to be a solemn and serious person, a man of few words, he was drastically mistaken. Burns not only stretched the story out with as much detail as possible — he even began acting out some scenes for his one-man audience.

Turning abruptly to one side, Burns became the hard-thinking chief telegrapher in Detroit. " 'Well, the writing does look familiar,' " he mimicked the man's voice. " 'But I'm positive it wasn't written by anyone working here now.' "

He spoke as himself again. "Now I was watching his face, and he was telling the truth. Besides, if he'd intended to lie, he'd have done it immediately. It's just common sense. He wouldn't have stared at the note so long first."

Burns went on to portray, in the same fully dramatized fashion, his interview with the chief telegrapher at the other Detroit station. And this time he imitated the look on the man's face when he saw the letter — surprise and then amusement. The telegrapher had promptly insisted he didn't recognize the printing. This was the giveaway.

Still playing both parts, Burns the Secret Service operative just as promptly accused Burns the second telegrapher of lying. The telegrapher had broken down then, admitting that the printing had been done by one of his men, but protesting that the fellow was just a blustering old Dutchman who really wouldn't put a bullet into anyone. After arresting and questioning the suspect, whose accent afforded an excellent opportunity for some dialect work in the staging of a climactic scene, Burns agreed. Thus the recommendation that the case be closed with a letter of apology.

"That was all there was to it," Burns concluded. "The whole thing was just common sense from beginning to end."

If Lord Julian Pauncefote saw any relation between the "just common sense," of William J. Burns and the "Elementary, my dear Watson," of the imaginary detective whose magazine-story exploits had been thrilling British readers for a dozen years, he was neither the first nor the last. Reporters had made the same comparison after listening to Secret Service Chief Wilkie's praise of Burns' work on the Pennsylvania counterfeiting case.   And by August of 1900, Assistant Attorney General James M. Beck would be writing Burns and expressing a "sincere belief that no detective, either of fact or fiction, ever surpassed . . . (your) wonderful intuition in divining the truth from apparently insufficient premises, worthy of the most subtle deductions of Sherlock Holmes."

Moreover, Burns had not yet reached the peak of his career.   Eleven years later, after he solved a mass-murder dynamiting case that probably created more headlines than any crime in American history, *The New York Times* would be calling him "the greatest detective certainly, and perhaps the only really great detective, the only detective of genius whom the country has produced."   On the far side of the Atlantic, even with Scotland Yard close at hand, the London *Spectator* could only turn again to fictional detectives to find counterparts for him:

> One likes to think of a detective as having a very distinguishing character of his own — the enduring criminal slyness of the reformed Vidocq, the kindliness of Bucket, or the deductive logic of Sherlock Holmes . . . Mr. Burns, personal appearance, we are told, is "a perfect disguise in itself," and "the outward habit of his mind is as good as an alias." He is "red" and "brisk" and rather small and has the appearance of "a prosperous businessman."
>
> So far as we can gather, he lives in the glare of publicity . . . When he walks abroad, he is followed by a small army of reporters to see what he does. Apparently all this is a mask, behind which the real detective works. It is an attractive notion — this of the detective pursuing secrecy in publicity and jovially allowing his

17

footsteps to be dogged by the more conventional amateur detectives of the press.

Noting that publications all over the world were deciding that "Mr. Burns is less like a detective than any detective who ever lived," the *Spectator* asked the essential question: "But what *is* a detective like?"

What William J. Burns was like can be answered many ways. Historically, he was the man who earned an incomparable reputation in the Secret Service, went on to become President Theodore Roosevelt's domestic Big Stick in a campaign against the public-lands thieves of the west, commanded a celebrated graft investigation in San Francisco, then founded and served as the star performer of the highly successful William J. Burns International Detective Agency. He closed his public career as J. Edgar Hoover's predecessor, heading what is now the Federal Bureau of Investigation for a brief time in the controversial and still-mystifying Harding era.

Personally, he was a man of strong opinions with no hesitation about expressing them. Flamboyantly self-confident and totally extroverted, he was warmly loved and hotly hated, but never treated with indifference. Burns bore little resemblance to the classic storybook detectives and still less to the heroes of modern detective fiction. He occasionally carried a revolver, but there is no record that he ever fired one on a case.

Yet he fought far bigger battles than pistol duels as he lived out a life stranger than any author could contrive. The powerful union leader Samuel Gompers once tried to rally the entire American labor movement against Burns, but was left looking like a fool. The most famous of all American attorneys, Clarence Darrow, tangled with Burns as well, and ended up narrowly escaping prison in the most wince-provoking episode of his long career.

On the other hand, Burns narrowly missed being put behind bars at least once himself. He was accused, at various times, of everything from jury-tampering to kidnapping. Yet he didn't hesitate to lend his talents to an unpopular cause — and was almost killed when he sought to prove the innocence of Leo Frank, a Jewish factory manager in the South whom large segments of the population believed guilty of murder and were determined to lynch.

William J. Burns probably achieved greater prominence and influence than anyone of his calling before him or since. Yet as constantly, and pleasurably, as he sunned himself in the public spotlight and as many formidable enemies as he made, no hint of scandal ever touched his private life. There was but one woman for him, and he married her as a teen-ager.

Burns undeniably sought and enjoyed publicity, but his craving for front-page news space never really interfered with his work. He repeatedly delighted in impressing newsmen with the intricate reasoning that had gone into solving some success-ful case, then insisting, with exaggerated modesty, that it was all "Just common sense!" Still, since he had no formal train-ing in crime detection of any kind, his skill very probably was a rare and highly perfected form of common sense, combined with dogged perseverance and what was almost certainly a photographic memory.

Today, the crime lab has made a science of the art he perfected; and his successors, the 18,000 employed by the Burns organization of the present included, will find it hard to picture a time when detectives worked with their wits alone. But until detectives can work without them in an era far harder to picture, Burns' story should lose none of its freshness and meaning.

That story could start at any number of places and points in time — or with a curious coincidence. In the year 1853, two immigrants arrived in the United States, and some two decades later they both became independent businessmen in Columbus, Ohio, although they took radically different routes to get there. One was a 12-year-old Irish stowaway fleeing from both a harsh stepfather and a potato shortage. His name was Michael Burns. The other, tall and handsome and traveling first class, in his mid-20's but already a skilled master engraver, was a blond-haired German named Charles Ulrich.

Mike Burns' story might well have been written by Horatio Alger. Apprenticing himself to a Baltimore tailor, he worked long hours without pay, wore castoff clothes, slept on a bench in the shop, borrowed books from customers and neighbors and secretly educated himself by candle light. Before long, he had learned enough to duck out of his apprenticeship and talk his way into a paying job as a journeyman tailor. Then he married Bridget Treahy, also recently from Ireland, and began a family immediately. Shortly after their first son, William John, was born in October of 1858, the couple moved west to Zanesville, Ohio. Six years later, Mike became the junior partner at the tailor shop of Dennis & Burns, and by 1873 he was ready to take his wife and six children on to Columbus and set up his own business.

Charlie Ulrich's chronicle was something else entirely. He had scarcely debarked from the boat when he fell in with a friendly fellow known as "Key Jim" Colbert, who casually suggested, over many mugs of beer, that the best way for an engraver to make money in America was to do so literally. Charlie just couldn't refuse a friend, so he went to work and turned out a perfect set of plates for a state bank note. But before the pair was able to spend a single bill they had printed, the authorities had them both behind bars. As a first offender, Charlie received only a two-year sentence, but he was still somewhat discouraged by the New World's lack of hospitality. So upon his release he enlisted in the English equivalent of the Foreign Legion and was off to the Crimean War.

With his broad shoulders and his fair curly hair, he cut a fine figure in a cavalryman's uniform as he rode in the famed "Charge of the Light Brigade" at Balaklava that offered such an inspiration to the poet Tennyson. But all the charge offered Charlie was a chance to get his skull cracked by a musket butt and have a Russian bayonet driven into his side. Left for dead on the battlefield, he lay there 36 hours before the British recovered the ground and carted him off to a field hospital. Discharged with some medals, persistent headaches and an occasional twinge in his ribs, he forgave the United States for the previous reception he'd received and sailed into New York a second time.

Still, he again took the promise of the Golden Door too literally. When a bogus-bill passer named Jim Courtney hunted him up and made the same suggestion that Colbert had offered, Charlie shook his head stubbornly. But he hadn't yet learned to refuse a lady, much less a pair of them. When Courtney found two buxom German girls named Kate Gross and Mary Braun and had them go to work on the reluctant engraver, Charlie was helpless. Once again he made up a set of plates, and once again was caught almost immediately.

Faced with a much longer prison term for his second offense, Charlie lost his usual philosophical resignation while brooding about the vagaries of life at Crow Hill Penitentiary in Brooklyn. So he studied the shape of the key the guard carried, cut a similar one from an iron washbasin with a common awl, then escaped across the border into Canada. There he again ran into his first partner in crime, Key Jim Colbert.

Key Jim was getting homesick, so he wrote a letter to the U.S. Secret Service, offering to turn Charlie in if he himself would be given a pardon in return. The Secret Service had to accept such offers. Men with an inclination toward counterfeiting were plentiful, but men with the skill to cut plates were few. The best way of keeping bad money out of circulation was to keep as many engravers behind bars as possible. So Charlie Ulrich, enjoying a peaceful game of pool one afternoon, had his recreation interrupted by a group of law-and-order guardians representing two nations.

This time, before tossing him into a Canadian prison, authorities carefully searched him for anything from which he could fashion a key. But they couldn't take his powerful shoulder muscles away. One day he managed to spread the bars of his cell wide enough to slip through. Then he scaled the prison wall by piling up buckets for a staircase. Guards saw him and opened fire, and in the excitement he got his foot firmly wedged in a bucket. But he tumbled on over and went clattering off into the darkness, losing both the bucket and his pursuers in a railroad yard. After hiding out for several days, he stole a rowboat one night and crossed back into the States. It wasn't until later that he learned he'd come within a few hundred yards of going over Niagara Falls.

Below the border, he discovered that his second partner in crime, Jim Courtney, was out on bond. He looked his good friend up in the hope of obtaining a small loan. Courtney stalled him, while doing exactly as Colbert had done. The big friendly engraver was offered to the Secret Service in return for a dismissal of the charges against Courtney. In 1867, Charles Ulrich began serving a 15-year sentence at the Ohio Penitentiary in Columbus.

Once again, he found himself an awl and a piece of steel — a circular saw blade that he smuggled back to his cell from the prison woodworking shop. But instead of cutting another key, he began work on a far more ingenious and perfectly legal escape plan. He engraved an extremely flattering likeness of Governor William Allen of Ohio, then asked the warden to present it to the governor as a present from a highly penitent penitentiary inmate. With each new admiring glance at the handsome profile so painstakingly etched in hard metal, Governor Allen became increasingly certain that a man with such a rare gift for reproducing reality deserved another chance.

As a result, not long after Irish tailor Michael Burns arrived in Columbus to establish his own business, Charles

Ulrich had a pardon in his pocket and was doing exactly the same thing.

There is no record that these two men ever as much as spoke to each other. The small side-street shop where the earthy ex-convict gulped back the temptation to pocket the rings and other pieces of jewelry upon which he inscribed initials and sentiments was some distance from the highly desirable location at the corner of High and Gay streets, where the dignified tailor's sign read, in tasteful simplicity, "BURNS." And even though Charlie reinforced his new respectability by marrying one of Columbus' ample supply of German girls and fathering a couple of daughters, he belonged to none of the civic service groups and Catholic layman's organizations in which Mike was active. But the eldest of the Burns boys stopped in often at the engraving shop. The former counterfeiter, with his talent for working miracles on metal and his colorful tales of prison breaks and distant battles, cut quite a figure in the eyes of any fellow in his early teens.

"Well," he would exclaim. "Bill Burns" (The way Burns imitated and perhaps exaggerated his accent later, it came out, "Vell, Pill Purns!")

Eventually, William J. Burns and Charlie Ulrich would get to know each other exceedingly well, but in those early days there was little to distinguish the future detective from other boys who came in to watch Charlie, or from Bill's classmates at the parochial and public schools he attended. He was a stocky, freckled redhead who, because of his father's trade, wore slightly better clothes than most Columbus youths, had a bit more spending money and less spare time. Michael Burns believed a few hours' work at the shop each day was good for his sons, although he had prospered well past the point of needing them.

Charles Ulrich left Columbus after a few years and went on to try his hand at manufacturing German pottery in New Jersey. And Bill Burns went on to high school, where he displayed a certain amount of theatrical talent. He loved to do dialect dramatizations, offstage as well as on, and the luckless counterfeiter he'd once known was one of the favorites in his repertoire.

Still small and redheaded, but with his freckles finally fading, Bill was remembered by those who knew him then as a fun-loving fellow whose practical jokes delighted his many friends and worried his father and teachers — almost a storybook stereotype of the popular, glib-tongued young Irishman. He was also captain of the school debating team, and Michael Burns wanted to send him to law school. Bill, working up a clog-dancing routine to go with his dialect comedy monologues, wanted to go on the stage — a notion designed to leave any respectable tailor red-faced and sputtering. Father and son finally agreed that Bill would take a business college course and then go to work at the tailoring shop.

In the meantime, though, Michael Burns had accepted the urgings of some fellow civic leaders and agreed to run for Police Commissioner on a reform ticket. He was elected, somewhat to his surprise, since Ohio politics in general and Columbus politics in particular were decidedly unreformed. Seventeen-year-old Bill Burns promptly took full advantage of his father's position by making himself at home around the police station, usually in the office of the two detectives on the 20-man force. Talk of crime and criminals still fascinated him as much as in the years when he'd listened to Charlie Ulrich's reminiscences.

He was doubtlessly regarded by the city detectives, at first, as a pest who had to be tolerated because his father was the commissioner. But his boyish interest in their work was both persistent and flattering, and he had become determined to make himself a valued, if unpaid assistant.

One time, a series of burglaries erupted that had the police completely puzzled. Six of Columbus' better homes were plundered in a single night. About two weeks later, exactly the same thing happened again. The detectives were certain the burglar had to be someone from out of town; a local man, they reasoned, would break into but one house at a time and not run such a risk.

Strictly on his own, Bill Burns went out and interviewed each of the burglary victims, then came back arguing that the culprit was a Columbus man. All of the homeowners had been off on trips, he pointed out, and all had had their travel plans mentioned on the society pages of the local newspapers.

Actually, his efforts played no part in solving the crimes. But when the troublesome second-story man was finally collared by a patrolman and proved to be a Columbus resident, Bill's ideas were taken more seriously at the station. Gradually, he earned himself a welcome that survived his father's term in office. The new commissioner, a former detective named Barney McCabe, was a friend and Bill continued to drop by when he had the chance.

By then, he had finished his business course and was working at his father's shop — relegating his frustrated theatrical ambitions to the founding of a local Shakespearean Society and the acting out of amusing stories for customers. And he had himself a steady girl — a slim, serious young lady from a German-Irish family, named Anna Maria Ressler.

The one word used most frequently in describing her, then and later, was "sensible." When she walked down the aisle to become Mrs. William Burns on July 5, 1881, she had a perfect picture of what lay ahead. She could be reasonably certain that Bill would father the sizable family she wanted and eventually become a full partner in his father's shop. By the time the tasteful sign said "BURNS & SON," Annie believed, Bill would have given up such things as the Shakespearean Society and hanging out at the police station and would be devoting his spare time to more meaningful community affairs. She expected Bill to follow in Michael Burns' footsteps, and she fully approved of the path.

This might very well have been the shape of their lives — if someone hadn't attempted to rig the local election of 1885.

On a Saturday night that October, with the vote counting still going on, the county clerk locked the tally sheets in his safe at the courthouse.   Unlocking that safe on Monday morning, he discovered that the results from Precinct A of the 13th Ward had been changed to give 300 more votes to each Democratic candidate.   The forgery was so skilled the clerk would have sworn the figures were his own, except that a slightly different shade of ink had been used.

Columbus was enraged.   The defeated county prosecutor, Robert Montgomery, who would have been re-elected had the fraud gone unnoticed, promised a prompt and thorough investigation.   But the forgery was still a mystery when Cyrus Huling, the new Prosecutor, took office at the turn of the year.   And the city detectives seemed content to let the matter rest.

Prosecutor Huling could understand their attitude. Columbus was normally Democratic territory, and no one could know how highly-placed those involved in the fraud might be. Career policemen had little taste for risking the wrath of men who might be returned to office in just a few years. So Cyrus Huling took an unusual step.   He dropped by the rented house on First Avenue where Bill and Annie Burns lived with their two children — three-year-old George Edward and one-year-old Charles Edwin — and asked the young tailor who still occasionally dropped in at the police station and played amateur detective if he'd care to turn professional on a spare-time basis.

Bill Burns jumped at the chance. Another child was expected, and Bill was able to point out to Annie that the extra money would be very welcome.   He could have added, but didn't, that he was so bored at the shop that he probably would have paid the prosecutor for the privilege of taking the job.

Burns began his first real case by analyzing the crime. Since the close Republican election victory had been a surprise forecast by nobody, it seemed highly improbable that the forgery was planned in advance. Far more likely, tampering with the tally sheets had been a desperation move decided upon only after the vote counting had begun and the trend was clear. So everything seemed to revolve around one troublesome question: where could a skilled forger and an expert safecracker be found in a hurry?

Pondering this problem, Bill began taking long walks and buggy rides in the evenings, mentally exploring every possibility, certain that the answer was escaping him only because of its sheer simplicity. One night he found himself staring at the sinister walls of the Ohio Penitentiary. "And there it was!" he'd chuckle years later, recreating the case as he always recreated his cases. "Where else?"

He followed up his hunch by socializing with the prison guards the same way he had with the force at the police station, dropping in regularly at a small lunchroom and tavern the changing shifts frequented. His persistence was rewarded one evening when he heard several of the uniformed men chuckling over a ridiculous story a convict named Tom Campbell had blurted out in the aftermath of an epileptic fit.

"Says he forged those tally sheets last September" a guard related. "But the funny thing is where he says he did it — in the crazy ward of the prison hospital."

Bill Burns joined in the general laughter. "Sounds like he belongs there."

"That's what Doc Montgomery says." The guard nodded.

"Doc Montgomery?" Bill stopped laughing.

"The prison doctor. His brother used to be prosecutor."

This was interesting, even though convict Campbell sullenly denied everything when Burns had Prosecutor Huling question him. A quick check of the prison files showed that one of Dr. Montgomery's helpers was a trustee named John

27

Francis, one of the most sensitive-fingered safecrackers in the business. Francis didn't deny anything; he offered, in fact, to tell the whole story of the election fraud. In return, he demanded a full pardon, but this was a price that the authorities simply wouldn't meet.

Even so, all signs now pointed strongly to the involvement of former prosecutor Robert Montgomery. Burns remembered that a clerk named Chase had quit his job in the prosecutor's office and disappeared just after the election. Some digging into police records revealed that the absent Mr. Chase was really one Algernon Granville of Chicago, a graduate of the Ohio Penitentiary himself. At this point, Bill decided to take a vacation from the tailoring shop and pay a visit to Chicago. It took a week of methodically checking hotels and other lodgings, but he finally found the clerk in an out-of-the-way boarding house.

"John Francis is willing to talk," Burns explained, truthfully, "but he wants both immunity from prosecution on this charge and a commutation of the sentence he's serving now. We'll meet his terms if we have to," he added, less truthfully, "but we'd naturally rather deal with you and offer only immunity."

Algernon Granville remained silent and suspicious.

"We only need one state's witness," Burns said. "And if Huling has to give Francis a pardon, he'll be angry enough about it to demand the fullest penalty for all others involved." In a very matter-of-fact manner, he left the address of his hotel and started out. He almost got to the bottom of the boardinghouse stairs before Granville called him back. The bluff had worked.

According to the account of the forgery attempt Burns heard from Granville then, Robert Montgomery had come up with the scheme after a frantic conference on election night with a few other office holders as the disturbing returns were being tabulated. After the ballots were locked up, Montgomery had his prison-doctor brother slip convict Francis out to

28

open the courthouse safe. Meantime, Granville went to the penitentiary and joined convict Tom Campbell at the hospital. When the prosecutor showed up a short time later with seven or eight tally sheets, the old figures were eradicated with acid. Then expert-forger Campbell penned new ones in the county clerk's handwriting. Returning the sheets to the safe on Sunday night was no problem; the courthouse watchman had been bribed.

Political influence being what it was, Algernon Granville would repeat this story to three successive grand juries before an indictment was returned and despite the ironclad evidence, the sensation-filled trial that followed two years later ended inconclusively when a pair of jurors the newspapers described as "highly suspect from the beginning" held out for acquittal. But as far as most of Columbus was concerned now, Bill Burns had solved the case, and his part in the affair was a decided success.

"Imagine rigging an election in the insanity ward of a prison hospital" he was still exclaiming when friends dropped in to admire his new son, Raymond Joseph. "Remember old Charlie Ulrich, who used to run the engraving shop and tell about his counterfeiting days? I'll be able to match the best of his yarns if I ever run into him again."

Running into Charlie seemed somewhat unlikely. The big German had lost interest in the New Jersey pottery business, backsliding into a more direct way of making money and ending up with a new 15-year sentence that was suspended through the pleas of his family and his own promise to leave the country. Returning to his homeland, he had established himself in Danzig as an importer of bargains, and had done a remarkably large-scale business. But as he attempted to get a well-earned rest by taking his family on a vacation trip to Switzerland, the authorities stopped him at the border, relieved him of some $200,000, and tossed him in prison. No one believed him, it seemed, when he insisted that absent-mindedness alone was responsible for his failure to pay for any of the vast quantities of goods he'd been selling at such attractively low prices.

The veteran rogue had gained a certain celebrity by then, and accounts of his European adventures appeared in New York newspapers along with the latest developments in the Ohio tally-sheets scandal. But Bill Burns probably first learned of Charlie's troubles in the spring of 1887, when Mrs. Ulrich brought her two daughters back to Columbus and began taking in washing to support them. Burns, however, had little time to worry about his old hero's latest misfortunes that year. His success in solving the forgery mystery was bringing him as much part-time detective work as he could handle, including one fairly lucrative theft case for a corporation. And to all who knew him, it was obvious that he was delighting in his new role.

His father was far from delighted. Private investigators already were known as "gumshoes." Proper folk regarded them, often deservedly, as a breed sometimes a slight step above criminals themselves and sometimes not. As it became even clearer that Bill intended to join their ranks and make a permanent practice of snooping into the affairs of forgers, embezzlers and other such people, Michael Burns had increasingly harsh words to say.

Annie Ressler Burns said little. Overwhelmed by her husband's new enthusiasm, by the unmistakable sense of vital function and aptitude he'd found for himself, there was little she could say. But the perfect picture she'd carried to the altar with her was dimming ominously.

That picture faded completely late in 1888, just after Annie's first daughter, Florence, was born. Bill left the tailoring shop and set himself up as a full-time private investigator — receiving most of his assignments from the Furlong Agency of St. Louis and serving something of an apprenticeship under its owner, a veteran detective named Tom Furlong.

Burns' life became a succession of train rides and rented

buggies, cheap hotels and tasteless meals, as he followed bad-check writers and swindlers and missing husbands about the entire Midwest. The everyday routine of his family went on largely without him. Usually he was able to get back to Columbus only between cases, though one day, he dropped a case and rushed back to be at the bedside of little Charles Edwin, who died of diptheria in 1890 — a loss partially eased by the birth of another boy named William Sherman early the following year.

Michael Burns never completely gave up hope that his eldest son would come to his senses and return to the respectability of the family business. But although there was a BURNS & SON sign on the shop when the immigrant tailor died in 1892, the son was James Henry, a year younger than Bill. On December 5, 1891, William J. Burns, at 33 years of age, had become an Assistant Operative of the United States Secret Service, for a salary of $3.00 a day.

As a private investigator, Burns had seen the seamier side of a detective's life. Now he learned its duller aspects. He received the normal promotion to Special Operative after slightly more than a year, with a pay raise to $4.00 a day, but his earliest government assignments were usually nothing more than attempts to back-trace bad bills through successions of people who had passed them on. Every so often, however, his senses were challenged by the excitement that had led him into detective work in the first place. His best remembered case from this period, in fact, was a postman's holiday of sorts, when he obtained a leave of absence from the Secret Service to help his former employer Tom Furlong break a St. Louis arson ring, headed by a brutal character named Jim French. To gather evidence, Burns concealed his identity and became a trusted friend of some of the arsonists. It was Burns' first close brush with danger. After the detective's testimony before the grand jury in closed session, a gang member named Rudd was found beaten to death behind a tavern, evidently in the belief that he was the informer.

With Burns still around and talking, ringleader French was sentenced to ten years in prison in January of 1894, and convictions of the others soon followed.

Bill Burns' visits to Columbus during those years are still remembered as memorable occasions by his surviving children. He would have presents for all, and give fascinating dramatizations of incidents and characters he had encountered in his travels. When he presided at his table, no matter what the menu, the meal became a banquet, with his flowery talk and his ceremonious mannerisms.

Even so, Annie Ressler Burns was rearing her family largely alone. Her picture of life with a prominent merchant tailor's son was practically forgotten. The only picture she and her children had of her husband, for weeks and sometimes even months at a time, was the bust portrait of him that hung in the hallway. This portrait prompted little Bill Sherman to add a wry, early touch to the Burns legend. "I do too have a daddy," he told his friends. "Only he just doesn't have any legs."

The Secret Service, throughout its 30-year history as an arm of the Treasury Department had been guided by six "General Orders." The first read, "Each man must recognize that his service belongs to the government through 24 hours of every day." The second added, "All must agree to assignment to the locations chosen by the Chief and must respond to whatever mobility of movement the work might require." Only an operative's wife could know just how literally those orders were taken.

The only semblance of a second honeymoon Annie Burns had was a Secret Service stakeout. Bill came home abruptly in November of 1894 to tell his wife to leave the school-aged children with her parents, then pack up Sherman and come to Cincinnati with him. Charlie Ulrich had been released from prison in Germany, had somehow slipped back into the United States unnoticed, and was once again making himself the proper concern of the U.S. Secret Service.

Burns checking courtroom transcripts

Annie Ressler Burns

George Burns

The authorities were certain Ulrich was planning to contact a big New York counterfeiting ring headed by William "Long Bill" Brockway, one of the most notorious criminals of the day, and would soon be cutting plates for them. Ulrich, now almost 70, had been traced to Cincinnati, where he evidently had joined his wife. But the wary old engraver had yet to show himself on the street. Secret Service operatives had noticed a "For Rent" sign in the window of a second-story flat directly across the street from Mrs. Ulrich's. But they had no doubt that Charlie had noticed it too and would become extremely suspicious if one or more single men moved into a neighborhood composed almost exclusively of young workingclass families.

Bill Burns had not only volunteered for the surveillance but had offered Annie and little Sherman as well. He assured his superiors that Ulrich would never connect the young family man across the street with the boy he had known so long before in Columbus. The assignment was his.

The new tenants on the block must certainly have seemed normal enough to their neighbors. Watches could have been set by the mustached fellow who emerged from the apartment building promptly at 6:30 each morning wearing a denim coat and cap, then walked briskly off swinging his lunch bucket. No one saw him circle a few blocks, then slip back through the alleys to relieve his wife, keeping watch at the front window.

"Anything happen?" he'd ask.

"Someone watched you walk off," Annie would tell him, sitting well back in the room as he'd taught her. "I think they're looking up here from time to time." Then she would get on with making breakfast and doing a morning's housecleaning, ready to drop everything and become an unpaid Secret Service operative again whenever her husband left.

After the first week or so, the wariness in Ulrich's flat seemed to be relaxing; the window curtains no longer parted

33

each time Bill set out with his lunch bucket. Then a day came when Charlie finally ventured out onto the street, evidently satisfied that his new neighbors were all that they appeared to be. His hair was a little whiter, Bill Burns decided as he shadowed the tall figure, but otherwise the man hadn't changed much; he still looked more like a college professor than a counterfeiter.

Almost daily, after that, Burns followed the old engraver on strolls about the city. He discovered, with wry delight, that advanced age had neither diminished the engraver's charm nor his vigor. "The old man," he told Annie with a grin, "has a lady friend on Vine Street." But apart from these amatory adventures, there was nothing significant or suspicious to report about Ulrich's trips away from home.

The days stretched into months. Annie didn't mind. She realized that this was the longest period she and her husband had been together in several years. There were moments, she later recalled, when she actually felt the part she was playing — that of a normal woman who got her man off to work each morning and had him home with her each night.

All through November and December, then January and February and March, the surveillance went on. Then one April morning, as Burns was keeping watch, Annie came in from the kitchen.

"I wish you'd bring in some coal," she told him.

He nodded and rose, offering her the chair and waiting until she had taken his place before starting back for the rear room where coal was kept. He had loaded but one lump in the bucket when he heard her call out.

"There he goes. Toward downtown."

She heard her husband drop the scuttle and rush to the closet for his coat and hat. Then the sound of his footsteps faded as he hurried down the back stairs to the alley.

She'd had Bill at home for more than five months. She had no way of knowing that she wouldn't see him again for another five.

34

After Ulrich left his lady friend's that morning, Burns sensed that the break he'd been awaiting so long might have come. The old counterfeiter immediately went through a succession of shadow-shaking tricks — strolling about in a purposeless manner and then stopping suddenly around a corner to stand still and wait; catching a streetcar going in one direction and then switching to another bound the opposite way at the first stop. Charlie finally entered the downtown office of the Chesapeake & Ohio Railroad. He came out after a few minutes and hurried off. Instead of following, the Secret Service operative waited a while, then rushed into the office acting worried and out of breath.

"Has my uncle been here yet?" he gasped. "Tall old fellow, curly white hair, thick German accent?"

"You just missed him," the clerk said.

"Did he get both our tickets?"

"No, just one."

"It's my own fault," Burns nodded. "He must have thought I wasn't coming when I was late meeting him. Well, give me another one. I'll catch him on the train." Burns avoided the possibility of questions with a quick trip to the water cooler.

Reading his ticket, he learned he would be on his way to New York within the hour. He hurried directly to the station, boarded the train, then watched from a window as Charlie Ulrich arrived. Pretending to be waiting for someone, Ulrich deliberately made himself the last person through the gate before it was closed, confident then that no one was following.

During the train ride, Burns managed to sneak a glimpse into Ulrich's suitcase while the old man was away from his seat. When he found a full set of engraving tools and some bill-sized metal plates as well, he dispatched two telegrams — one telling Annie to move back to Columbus, the other a report to Secret Service Chief William P. Hazen. Another operative joined Burns at Philadelphia. Once they'd followed

Ulrich from the New York station to the nearest telegraph office and caught him in the act of contacting a member of the Brockway gang, the two Secret Service man identified themselves and arrested him. But instead of arranging with the New York police to have Ulrich booked and jailed, they took him, at Burns' suggestion, to a private room at the St. James Hotel.

"Don't you remember me, Charlie?" he finally asked.

Ulrich shook his head, looking puzzled.

"Remember the engraving shop you had in Columbus? I used to go there and watch you work. My name's Burns. Bill Burns."

The old German remembered then, grinning and shaking hands heartily. As casually as if this were a normal social occasion, Burns ordered and ample supply of cold beer. With nostalgia steadily increasing the counterfeiter's thirst, detective and suspect reminisced pleasurably for a long time. Then Burns turned thoughtful and shook his head sadly. "When was it they first landed you, Charlie? Back in '56, wasn't it? You were let off easy, went away to war, came back and got into trouble again first thing. Who was it turned you in up in Canada?" The question was rhetorical; Burns long ago had memorized every detail of Ulrich's record. "Key Jim Colbert, wasn't it?"

The engraver nodded, his grin fading with the memory.

"So you got away again, ducked back down to the States, and what happened? Jim Courtney turned you in."

"Courtney." Ulrich agreed bitterly.

"It was a succession of betrayals, Charlie," Burns reminded him. "There was never a man yet who profited by your work who ever did anything for you in return." Burns hammered at this point for some time, then turned to a new attack. "Think of your wife, taking in washing and ironing, cleaning other women's houses all day and her own half the night, working early and late. She brought those girls of yours up right, though, didn't she? But you, you never gave a thought to those girls. Those girls just becoming women now. It doesn't bother you to have them pointed out on the street as the daughters of a notorious counterfeiter, does it?"

It did bother Charlie. Sentimental by nature and on his seventh or eighth mug of beer by then, he had tears in his eyes. "What's the use of reminding me?" he kept protesting.

"You need to be reminded," said Burns, remorselessly. "Those girls of yours will be getting married soon. You'll have grandchildren, but you'll never see them. There's still that 15-year suspended sentence hanging over your head in Jersey, you know. And now the Brockway bunch." He shook his head in disgust. "Bill Brockway — who's kept out of prison a half-dozen times by turning in every engraver who ever worked for him. That's the kind of man you place above your own family."

A good detective had to be something of a psychologist, and Bill Burns was well on his way to becoming a very good detective. He hammered away at Ulrich's foolishness in a dozen different ways and then, very gradually, offered a few hints that it might not be too late after all. The purpose, of course, was to get Charlie Ulrich to work as a Secret Service informer. When the old engraver finally agreed, he was turned loose to contact the Brockway gang as he had originally intended, and to make regular reports to Bill Burns.

After entertaining Charlie lavishly for a time, the counterfeiters suddenly spirited him off to New Jersey and kept him a virtual prisoner at an old house there while he worked on the plates they wanted. But he still managed to smuggle out messages, mentioning the location of incriminating evidence. On August 3, 1895, Burns, another agent, and Chief Hazen himself raided the house and made the first arrests in a series that ended on September 7 with every member of the gang behind bars.

It proved to be Burns who came up with the vital piece

of evidence that brought ringleader Brockway to justice. In going over the contents of the New Jersey hideaway, Burns found a homemade oilcloth apron. Brockway had a reputation for covering his tracks well. He denied ever having been in the Jersey house, and there was no proof to the contrary, until Burns spotted a strangely shaped oilcloth in William Brockway's own home. The cloth had a gap into which the apron fitted perfectly.

Even then, the Ohio operative's work on the case was far from finished. Star witness Ulrich had to be guarded. His life was being threatened by anonymous notes. Burns was given the job of keeping him safe until the Brockway gang could be forced to trial. When Bill was given leave to visit his family, he had to take Charlie with him. On returning to active duty, he was sent to Florida to keep watch on some Cuban revolutionaries. The old counterfeiter came along. While Bill was off listening at café tables, Charlie amused himself by swindling an elderly German couple out of their $2500 savings — a scheme Burns discovered just in time to force the return of the money. Bill hurried home to Columbus when his mother died that December and stayed on through the Christmas season. With the new year just four days old, Annie gave birth to their second daughter and fifth living child, Kathleen. And a nationally notorious counterfeiter was still their house guest.

When Burns finally delivered Ulrich safely to the witness stand in mid-February, the old man's testimony proved worth all the trouble. He told his story clearly and precisely, refusing to waver in the slightest under a vehement cross-examination. On March 8, William Brockway was sentenced to ten years in prison, with his confederates receiving lesser terms.

Charles Ulrich lived on for another dozen years, running a small engraving shop in Connecticut. Though his days of mischief were over, his reputation persists. To students of the counterfeiting art, he is generally regarded as the most highly skilled platemaker to plague the Secret Service up to the advent of photoengraving. Some of the incredibly delicate miniatures he made have been preserved by the Burns Agency to this day.

In closing the Brockway case, Chief William P. Hazen announced that "the Secret Service can rest easier now, having kept more than a half-million counterfeit dollars out of circulation." And on May 2, 1896, William J. Burns was promoted to full operative, with a pay raise to $6.00 a day. He was permanently transferred to the New York district as well, but there was little as yet to distinguish him from his fellow Secret Service men. He was energetic and capable; he made some brilliant deductions on occasion. But so did Schuyler Donella, Frank Esquirell, W. J. McManus, Tom Callaghan, W. J. Flynn, and a long list of now-forgotten others with whom he worked. Not until Burns was almost 39 and a veteran of six years in government service did he get a case that showed the more sensational kind of work he was capable of doing.

On April 14, 1897, in the small Central American country of Costa Rica, a customs inspector named Gerado Yglesias ran first a critical eye and then an experienced pair of hands over a burlap-wrapped sofa that had been unloaded from an Atlas Line ship onto the Port Limón docks. There was nothing really unusual about the appearance of this particular piece of furniture, except that it was wrapped a bit more heavily and carefully than usual. Yglesias ordered the burlap removed but saw no suspicious bulges. Then he began pressing his fingers into the upholstered back. Sensing an almost intangible variation in the response of the padding, he slit a seam and spread it.

Nearly a million pesos in counterfeit Costa Rican currency spilled out.

The sofa was cheap and old and contained no identifying marks beyond a faint "XX1634" on its burlap covering.

According to the bill of lading, it had come from the New Manhattan Chair Company of New York, which it turned out didn't exist, and was destined for one Santo Compo at the Imperial Hotel in San José. Senor Compo did exist and was promptly arrested, tried and convicted. But he stubbornly claimed he was the victim of a plot and refused to say who in the United States was making counterfeit pesos and sending them to him.

There was little more Costa Rica could do but notify Washington. Secret Service Chief Hazen promptly ordered Operatives Owens and Lutz to catch the next ship out of New Orleans and make an on-the-spot investigation. Also assigned to the case but without benefit of a Central American voyage, Operative Bill Burns was given the piece of old burlap containing the faded label and told to see what he could do with it.

At first, it seemed that nothing could be done. When Burns checked with major burlap manufacturers, he learned that "XX1634" wasn't even a burlap brand.

"Most of our production is sold to other factories," one manufacturer explained. "They use it for wrapping shipments they send to wholesale and retail outlets. The burlap is stamped with a shipment number that identifies the product inside. The outlets often use the burlap to protect late shipments of their own, or sell it to their customers. Most burlap you see has been used at least once."

This meant the "XX1634" could designate any type of article that might be wrapped in burlap. And Burns soon discovered that "XX" brands were a favorite in numerous lines of merchandise. Nevertheless, he went on working at what seemed an impossible task — compiling lists of factories that shipped their products in burlap and checking them out as rapidly as possible. When he'd exhausted the possibilities in New York City, he moved upstate. After weeks of work, with hundreds of fruitless queries behind him and possible thousands ahead, he visited a small manufacturer of work clothes at Newburgh, New York.

"Did this come from your plant?" He methodically displayed the piece of burlap.

"I think it might have," the owner finally decided.

"If it did, what would the '1634' stand for?"

"If it's ours, that's the order number."

"Would the order show who bought the goods wrapped in this particular piece of burlap?"

"If it could be found, it would," the plant owner said. But he then explained that he didn't have space to keep old orders filed. Except for the current year's records, everything was simply crammed into a small storeroom. He opened a door and pointed to dusty, yellowed heaps of paper 12 and 14 feet high. "There must be 20,000 orders there. I've been intending to have them cleaned out and burned." He started to close the door again.

"Mind if I try looking anyway?" Bill Burns asked.

The man gave him a surprised look, shrugged and left. Burns was not being stupidly persistent. He knew that some semblance of order had to exist in those mountains of sales forms, if only because records from any given period would probably have been discarded at about the same time, with certain traces of the system under which they had originally been filed remaining. He spot-checked the numbers on the top sheets, compared the aging of the paper, and finally picked out what seemed the most likely place to start. Then, working like a prospector following the color of ore, he started digging.

Two hours later, with dust coating his clothes and perspiring skin alike, he emerged with a single sheet of paper and hurried to better light to study the almost indiscernible scribbling on it. Order #1634 had been a shipment of overalls sold to a dry goods house in Long Island City, across the East River from Manhattan.

Early the next morning, Burns walked into the store and asked for burlap to wrap some furniture. The salesman on the main floor haughtily directed him to the basement, where the cheaper materials were sold, and turned him over to a young stock boy.

"How mucy do you want?" the fellow inquired.

Burns pretended to be pondering the question while actually sizing the boy up. Satisfied that the youngster would keep his confidence, Burns presented his credentials. "I'm looking for someone who was in here buying burlap a few months ago," he said, "probably a Spanish-looking man."

The boy was thrilled with the thought of assisting the Secret Service. He ticked off the various men he recalled who had bought burlap, but he could remember no one answering the description. "There was a lady, too," he added as an afterthought. "A little old lady all dressed in black and wearing a shawl. She had gold-rimmed glasses on. I remember her very well."

This sounded like the way elderly Latin ladies frequently dressed. Burns thanked the stock boy, then started on a task that seemed as improbable as tracing the label — finding the right little old lady. He knew that unless she lived relatively close, he had almost no chance. But he casually inquired around Long Island City, and was lucky. A Mrs. Chavin, who answered the description, kept house for her son-in-law at 66 Fourth Street.

During his next lunch hour, the stock boy walked with Burns to that address.

"No need for you to say anything," the Secret Service man explained. "Just take a good look."

Burns knocked on the door. When it opened, he tipped his hat and genially inquired if a woman whose name he quickly made up lived there.

"There is no one of that name," an accented elderly lady told him.

Burns apologized politely, walked off, then turned to his companion.

"That's her." The boy nodded emphatically.

A little old lady seemed an extremely unlikely exporter of counterfeit pesos. But Burns began making inquiries of furniture movers beginning with those nearest the Chavin home. He eventually came across an express-wagon driver who remembered carting an old sofa from the Fourth Street address to the Atlas Line docks. The questioning of a long succession of longshoremen came next. A man named Otto Haake not only recalled loading the sofa but was also certain he could identify a handsome dark-haired fellow who had watched the process and constantly irritated the workmen by urging them to be careful.

The dark-haired fellow, Burns discovered without difficulty, was Mrs. Chavin's son-in-law, a 40-year-old widower named Ricardo de Requesans. A few more inquiries and the Secret Service operative learned that de Requesans had made a trip to Costa Rica just a short time before the peso-packed sofa had been discovered. He'd traveled with an attractive lady, and they had signed themselves Emil and Eugenia Reinemann. Since this proved to be the lady's real name, Burns found her easily — a 36-year-old widow living in a New York City residential hotel at 153 West Fourteenth Street.

Burns had read an amazing amount of information from a faded label. After studying his reports, Secret Service Chief Hazen had a quick exchange of wires with Operatives Lutz and Owens in Costa Rica, then ordered de Requesans and Mrs. Reinemann arrested on June 3. The next morning, with the pair lodged in New York's Ludlow Street jail and protesting their innocence, the Chief took the strange step of admitting to reporters that he as yet had no real evidence that could convict the prisoners in court. He was certain, he explained, he would have an ironclad case when his men brought back witnesses they had located in Costa Rica.

Burns, who wasn't privileged to read the Chief's telegrams, had no reason to question this prediction. Since he was given no new assignments, he merely went on building his own case, hoping to help Lutz and Owens when the prisoners came to trial. Counterfeiters often kept their plates hidden instead of destroying them, then used them to bargain for lighter sentences if they were caught. Now Burns revealed a hidden talent of his own. He studied Ricardo de Requesans' handwriting, carefully forged a note from him to his mother-in-law — telling her to get the plates and keep them in a safe place — and had a trustee smuggle the message to Mrs. Chavin the next time she visited the jail.

He followed as the black-shawled lady went directly to her home in Long Island City. Ducking around to a back window, he saw her get a large handbag and leave it on the dining room table. When she went upstairs, he slipped in, found the bag empty, then slipped out and waited again. The lady led him back to New York, to the Spanish-American Printing Company at 126 Maiden Lane.

Inside, she approached a man Burns later learned was a lithographer named Herman Dohn. The detective couldn't get close enough to hear their voices, but he could see Dohn shaking his head and looking puzzled while the old woman seemed to become increasingly furious. Finally, she stalked out and went home, with no counterfeit plates in her handbag.

It appeared to be another dead end until Burns investigated the printing plant and discovered that Mrs. Reinemann and Ricardo de Requesans were the owners. Every bit as interesting, he learned that the chief product of the company was Spanish-language revolutionary literature which supported the ambitions of a self-styled "General," Frederico Mora, an exiled Costa Rican who had long been spawning schemes for a coup in his homeland. Furthermore, Mora lived at the same hotel as Mrs. Reinemann and had been closely associated with de Requesans for years — all of which seemed to add up to a plot for financing the overthrow of the Costa Rican government with fake pesos.

Burns had no real proof of this, of course, and when Owens and Lutz arrived in New York with six Costa Rican witnesses on June 15, they added nothing to any potential case against Mora and very little that could implicate the man and woman already jailed. Just what sort of misunderstanding had occurred in the exchange of telegrams, Burns never knew. But it turned out that the Latin witnesses could testify to little more than the fact that Mrs. Reinemann and de Requesans had been seen talking to Santo Compo, the man for whom the sofa was destined, and to a hotel waiter who had also been connected with the counterfeit currency. Such evidence could never bring an arraignment, much less a conviction, and the arrests Chief Hazen had ordered had been incredibly premature. Hazen and the entire Secret Service were in serious trouble unless Burns' theory was correct and could be proven. Returning to the Spanish-American Printing Company, Burns questioned all of the employees vigorously. He discovered that the puzzled look on the face of lithographer Herman Dohn had been genuine. Mrs. Chavin had gone to the wrong Dohn. Dohn's son William finally broke down and confessed engraving the counterfeit plates, working futively at night for the company's two owners. When those plates were recovered from the bottom of the river where the younger Dohn had thrown them, the Secret Service could take a deep breath; the evidence against Mrs. Reinemann and de Requesans was firm enough to offer any jury.

But there was still nothing to implicate their associate, the revolutionary leader Frederico Mora. This man was so confident, in fact, that he called at the Secret Service office, mentioned that he understood he was being investigated and offered to cooperate in any way he could. ("He was a real gentlemen," Bill Burns later recalled. "And if it served his purpose, I think he would have slit a throat and sunk a ship without the slightest hesitation.")

However, several personable young men of the Secret Service were already working on the jailed Mrs. Reinemann — suggesting that she had been treated somewhat less than gallantly by her Latin lover and hinting she could still escape prison by turning state's evidence against him, particularly if she could offer convincing testimony against Mora as well. Was it fair, this widow was asked again and again, for the cunning plotter who'd used her to go free, while she herself went to the penitentiary?

Eugenia Reinemann, whom the newspapers called "more than good looking," was soon telling her entire story. She'd been supporting both of these suave, handsome gentlemen for many months in the belief that once Frederico Mora succeeded with his counterfeit-financed revolution, Ricardo de Requesans would marry her and be appointed the Costa Rican Consul General at New York, where she would then live in style as a diplomatic hostess.

On October 26, 1897, the two Latin adventurers were brought to trial, and just four days later, both were sentenced to two years in Sing Sing. But the testimony of the man who had dug up the entire case against them from nothing more than a faint label on a piece of old burlap wasn't needed in court. In fact, William J. Burns was out in rural Indiana at the time — selling life insurance.

A month and a half earlier, on September 14, a mob of masked men had forced their way into the Ripley County jail at Versailles, Indiana — shooting three prisoners, dragging two more from their cells alive, then hanging all five from a limb of a giant oak on a bluff locally known as Gordon's Leap. A grand jury had investigated the matter, but with sentiment solidly on the side of the lynchers, no indictments had been returned. Governor James A. Mount had appealed to the U. S. Attorney General, and Secret Service Chief Hazen had been called in.

Technically, the sole proper concern of the Secret Service was counterfeiting. (Not until 1901, after McKinley became the third President to be assassinated in office, did Congress consider Presidents needed guarding and turn the job over to the Secret Service.) But actually the Treasury agency had of necessity handled every kind of assignment for which no other investigatory force existed — from involuntary-servitude cases through illegal lotteries to the attempted theft of Abraham Lincoln's bones from his tomb. And Operative Bill Burns was soon on his way westward with orders to attempt to learn the identity of a lynch mob's members in their own hostile, authority-defiant region.

Although the assignment was one that few of his fellow agents envied, it did give him a chance to stop off in Columbus and see his family on his way westward. His stays at home were infrequent and usually brief. In later years, his children would confess that they saw little of their father as they were growing up. When asked, though, what kind of parent he was, they would glow with pride. "He was a family man," they would reply in instant, emphatic unison. "Outside of his work, his family was his whole life." He arrived on this visit, as he usually did, with an armload of presents for Annie and the four children. Included was a large, extremely expensive doll for the baby Kathleen. (He never called her "Kathy," or her 9-year-old sister Florence "Flo." His nicknames ran in the opposite direction — "Madame Florenzio" or "Princess Magoosulum" for the baby.)

"Will," his wife reminded him when the doll was unwrapped, "she's not even two yet."

Burns blithely shrugged off her protests until the baby, slamming the doll on the floor, cracked its skull. Then he sorrowfully agreed it would have been a more suitable present for Florence. But if the detective was delightfully impractical in dealing with those he loved, he was deadly earnest as he thought of the business ahead. He had already evolved a plan for an entirely different kind of make-believe for use in Indiana.

At Indianapolis a few days later, he had a secret conference in the office of Attorney General Ketcham, and he was introduced to two men who had been assigned to help him with the investigation: a veteran U. S. Deputy Marshal named Ed Smith and a young detective named Steve Connell. Ketcham's assistant, Merrill Moore, filled the three of them in on the known details of the lynching.

A band of burglars had been terrorizing Ripley County — breaking into isolated farmhouses at night, torturing at least one elderly couple to learn where their valuables were, and committing "other heinous crimes," which meant they had molested some local women. Three suspects were captured — an elderly giant of a man named Lyle Levi, and two of his friends, Henry Schuter and William Jenkins. The Ripley County sheriff went after two more suspects, a pair of hoodlums named Andrews and Gordon, and was badly wounded in a gun battle with them. A group of armed citizens joined with deputies in running down the pair, while the sheriff lay wounded. The deputies who were guarding the jail blandly insisted afterward that they'd been helpless because their shotguns somehow had been unloaded that night, when men with handkerchiefs on their faces forced their way in, gunned down Levi, Schuter and Jenkins, then dragged out all five and strung them up.

Were any of the jail's prisoners spared? Burns wondered.

Just one, he was told, a boy named Kelly, who was now in the state reformatory. But no one had been able to learn anything from him. He had obviously been threatened and badly frightened, and it was quite possible that he had no useful information anyway.

Burns turned to the young detective, Steve Connell, and told him his job would be to enter the reformatory as an inmate and find out if Kelly did know anything.

"I don't know if I can do it," Connell protested. "Those reform school kids don't even shave yet."

"Then shave at night when no one's looking," Burns said.

Deputy Marshal Ed Smith was a tall, rawboned Missourian in his mid-50's. Burns decided that he should go into the farm-equipment business. From his private-detective days, Burns knew a Chicago manufacturer he was certain would do him the favor, at least temporarily, of establishing a new outlet in Ripley County. Farmers habitually liked to pass the time of day in machinery salesrooms, as well as in general stores. With no women around in the salesrooms, they talked more freely.

"A stranger opening a store in Versailles would create suspicion right now," he told Smith as they studied a map of the county. "Suppose you set up in the next town to the north — Osgood. When you hear anything worth passing on, don't take chances on any Ripley County post office. Drive all the way over to North Vernon in the next county to mail your reports."

Now Burns began his own part in the strategy. Introducing himself as "W.J. Burton" at the Indianapolis office of the New York Life Insurance Company, he asked for a job as a salesman. He was curtly informed the firm had all the salesmen it needed, until he mentioned that he was willing to work the hinterlands on a commissions-only basis. Then a sales manager, who clearly regarded him as not very bright, welcomed him heartily. So little insurance was being sold in the farm country that few salesmen were willing to waste time trying.

"What I would like to do first," Burns said, "is learn the business as thoroughly as possible."

Not until he'd mastered every bit of information about life insurance the Indianapolis office had to offer did he go on the road. And even then he worked his way toward Versailles in slow stages, knocking on doors in one county while mailing his promotion literature to the next, polishing his role to perfection in safe territory and advertising himself well in advance. In dozens of general stores and taverns, in hundreds of farmhouse parlors, he played the part of a disillusioned traveling man who had grown sick of city life and hotels and restaurant meals and was longing for the earthy joys of rural and small-town existence. His reputation spread. If he was not always welcomed, he was always believed.

Using county directories for his mailing lists and saturating every area with pamphlets before he entered it, he took several weeks to reach Ripley County — where practically every citizen knew by then that W. J. Burton of New York Life Insurance was coming. However suspicious the residents of the lynching area might be, none of them could accuse this particular stranger of attempting to sneak in. Burns' first stop in the county was Osgood. There, to the delight of lounging onlookers, he promptly tried to peddle a policy to the town's new farm-machinery dealer — a tall, laconic fellow who irritably insisted he needed no insurance and rapidly lost patience. The eager salesman persisted until a door was slammed in his face, and even then he insisted he was not discouraged.

"I'll sell that old mossback yet" he swore. "I'll be back."

He did come back — several times — as he solicited every possible prospect in the Osgood area. When he would return to the store and find no customers around, he picked up what information Deputy Marshal Smith had been able to gather from the talk he'd overheard. Smith was certain that men from all over the county — Osgood, Napoleon and Milan as well as Versailles — had been in on the lynching, and he had a few prime suspects to suggest. He'd also heard that the gun used to kill Lyle Levi was a .44 caliber revolver that had been borrowed from the window of McCoy's General Store in Osgood, then returned to the window, where it was still being offered for sale. But he didn't know who had taken the pistol.

All the answers, if they were to be found at all, seemed to be waiting ahead in Versailles. And Burns hired a boy with a wagon and an old white horse to drive him on down a dusty road that ran between fields of grain stubble and cut corn. The only hotel in Versailles was an ancient two-story building of whitewashed bricks on Main Street, with a tavern and a dining room on the first floor and sleeping rooms on the second.

The hotel fronted on the courthouse square. Any newcomer stepping down from a wagon in that setting might have felt that the entire community was watching him from all sides. In the case of the alleged insurance salesman, this was more than just a feeling. When he went inside to register, he wasn't exactly welcomed.

"The town is right shy of strangers now," the hotel owner told him. "Might be best to move on."

Burns acted puzzled.

"Didn't you hear what happened here last month?" The man eyed him evenly.

Bill Burns shook his head.

"Well, some men were strung up, and if anybody ever deserved hanging, it was them. But there's been snoopers comin' around stirrin' up trouble ever since. So why don't you hire a rig over at the livery stable and get out of here fast?"

"I've already sent my firm's advertising to this area," Burns said. "I can't waste an entire mailing."

The hotel owner shrugged and gave him a room. From its window, Burns noticed that the white horse and wagon were still in front of the building, surrounded by a group of men who were obviously questioning the driver. But this was to be expected. Washing a thick layer of dust from his face and hair and brushing another from his suit, Burns went down to an evening meal.

He ate alone, and when he entered the tavern afterward, a hush came over the place. Hostile stares burned into him from every table. His attempts to make the sort of small talk he'd made everywhere else on his Indiana tour brought only muttered replies and turned heads.

Finally, a grizzled tobacco-chewing character walked over and sat down with him — a liveryman from the local stable and very probably, from what Ed Smith had overheard at Osgood, one of the lynch-mob leaders. Obviously delegated to question him, the man made little attempt at hiding his hard-eyed skepticism.

How much did an insurance salesman make a year? the liveryman wondered. How much on each policy? How many folks did he usually have to call on before he found one who would buy? How long had W.J. Burton been in the business?

Burns pretended to be delighted to find someone so interested in his work. He launched into a fact-and-figure-filled dissertation on insurance designed to dull the senses of any listener.

"You thinking of going into the business yourself?" he asked presently.

"Might be," the fellow allowed, tight-lipped above his tobacco-stained whiskers. "Might be doing just that."

Burns leaned closer. "Then why not list some likely prospects for me?" he suggested in a low, confidential voice. "If any of them buys a policy, you'll get a cut of the commission."

The man seemed taken aback by the notion. Muttering that he'd think it over, he got up and left.

Indiana nights had turned cold, but Burns left his window open when he went to bed. Shortly after midnight he was roused by soft but quarreling voices below.

"We can't take any chances," someone was arguing. "He was warned not to stop here."

"Anything more happens," another voice countered, "and they'll be calling out the militia or something."

Burns had a small pistol in his coat pocket. But at least some of the half-dozen or more men in the darkness below were probably also armed, and there was an entire hostile town to be awakened by any commotion. He could do little but listen, wait and hope. The muted debate went on and on, most of it in whispers he couldn't hear. At last the sound of footsteps faded down the sidewalk boards.

In the morning he began working Versailles much the same way he'd worked all the other towns, calling first on such prominent citizens as a lawyer, a banker and a real estate broker, none of whom wanted any insurance. When he returned to the hotel, he found that his room had been searched and his mail had been opened. But this too had been expected. The belongings he'd left at the hotel were strictly those of any insurance salesman, and his mail was solely from the Indianapolis office of New York Life.

He spent the next few days soliciting the merchants of the town. During that time, he later discovered, there were inquiries about him with his insurance company. Moreover, some Versailles citizen evidently hired a real insurance salesman to check out Burns because another stranger showed up at the hotel one day. Introducing himself as being in the same business, he then spent the entire evening doing nothing but talking shop with Bruns, vanishing in the morning without any attempt to sell a policy.

When Burns began calling on the outlying farmers of the area, he hired the very liveryman who had questioned him the first night to take him around. Outlining a route west of Versailles, he mentioned that he wanted to swing north to Osgood later in the day. "There's an old hardhead running a machinery store there," he explained, "and I'm going to write a policy on him if it's the last thing I do."

He found Deputy Marshal Smith alone that day, but Smith couldn't add anything new. On the way back to Versailles, Burns noticed that the driver seemed to have something on his mind. Several times, the scowling, bearded man turned and seemed on the verge of saying something, but each time, he turned back to stare ahead in sullen silence. The town was in sight before he finally spoke up.

"Did you really mean it about cutting me in on the commissions if I gave you some tips?"

For the rest of Burns' stay in Ripley County, the liveryman had a steady stream of suggestions to offer — most of which were still in alphabetical order, having been copied directly from the county directory. And Bill Burns could sense Versailles slowly relaxing around him. He no longer caused a hush when he entered the tavern in the evening. By the end of his first week at the hotel, he was being invited to eat with the owner and his family. Then he even began to hear fragments of talk about the lynching.

He showed as much curiosity as he estimated any insurance salesman would show, no more and no less. Gradually, he learned how the Ripley County sheriff, although still stiff from his wound, had actually been back on his feet by the night of the lynching but had obligingly stayed in bed during the festivities. He learned how the five deputies assigned to guard the jail had indeed found their shotguns unloaded, having unloaded them themselves. At the end of about two weeks, Bill Burns had been accepted to such an extent that, when he mentioned he intended cutting a piece of bark from the hanging tree at Gordon's Leap, he was offered other souvenirs — one of the ropes used in the lynching and a handkerchief that had served as a mask.

When he finally said he had to leave — protesting, truthfully enough, that he hadn't sold enough insurance to justify a small fraction of the time he'd spent in the town — the new friends this genial fellow had made were genuinely sorry to see him go. At about the same time, a Chicago farm-machinery manufacturer decided to discontinue a recently-established Osgood outlet. And at the state reformatory, an inmate who seemed older than the rest was suddenly released. Meeting at Indianapolis, Burns, Smith and Connell combined their findings into a detailed report that identified all of the ringleaders of the lynch mob, a good share of its members and even some of the onlookers.

Attorney General Ketcham of Indiana sent the Secret Service a long, enthusiastic letter praising the report. But all of the imaginative, risky detective work was wasted in the end. The lynchers included key members of several Ripley County communities, and no local court would convict them. Once again, as with his first professional case, Bill Burns saw a successful investigation fail to bring about a successful prosecution.

By then, however, he had gone on to a still more challenging test of his skills. Even before he had left Versailles, in fact, he had heard of what was to be his next case. A bogus $100 bill had turned up that could make Charlie Ulrich's best efforts seem crude by comparison — a counterfeit so perfect that it had fooled every expert in the Redemption Division of the U.S. Treasury Department itself.

PART TWO

The Star of the Secret Service

One autumn day in 1897, a receiving teller of the subtreasury at Philadelphia was counting money — swiftly and expertly, wetting his finger from time to time as he went through thick stacks of bills. Suddenly he paused. With his finger freshly moistened, he had touched the carmine seal of a $100 "Monroe-head" silver certificate, and it had blurred, becoming almost illegible.

The teller knew that money wasn't intended to be water-proof, that water can cause the ink to run on legitimate currency — but not quite so readily. Staring at the suspect bill for a long time, he set it aside and later examined every detail with a microscope. But he could find no flaw beyond the smeared seal itself.

When he brought the matter to the attention of his superiors, they all agreed that the explanation was obvious: this was a genuine bill with a forged seal. Somehow, some-one had stolen a supply of $100 notes while they were on their way from the Bureau of Engraving and Printing to the Treasury to have seals added.

Instead of informing the authorities of the discovery of a counterfeit, the subtreasury officials sent the strange bill to Washington with a report that stated a seal had been forged on stolen currency. Secretary of the Treasury Lyman.

Gage immediately called the specialists of the Redemption Division into secret conference, with Chief William P. Hazen and Chief Clerk W. Herman Moran of the Secret Service present.

One by one, the experts subjected the note to every scientific test and examination in their repertoire. And one by one, they solemnly pronounced it genuine. Secretary Gage was deeply relieved; the theft of a small amount of authentic currency was a minor matter in comparison to the problem the finding of a near-perfect counterfeit would have posed. But Chief Clerk Moran then picked up the bill, studied it a moment and fingered it thoughtfully.

Would it be all right if he chanced ruining the bill with one more experiment? he asked.

The Redemption Division experts nodded and watched indulgently as Moran filled a paper cup from the water cooler, let the bill soak for a time, then began picking at one of the sodden corners with his thumbnail. To everyone's amazement, the $100 note came apart. It had been printed on three laminated sheets of paper, with silk threads inserted between. Not just the seal but the entire bill was counterfeit.

The gasp heard in that room echoed through the banking circles of the nation in an atmosphere bordering on panic. If a bogus bill could fool the Treasury Department, what chance would mere bank tellers have of recognizing the many others that were probably already in circulation? Was every such bill presented for payment to be soaked in water? Secretary Gage had absolutely no choice but to recall the entire $27 million Monroe-head issue.

Still in Versailles, Indiana, at the time, William J. Burns learned of this startling discovery by the same means as practically everyone else in the country — the local newspaper. Through the night that followed, he got less sleep than he had the night a group of lynchers had gathered outside his hotel-room window.

If the $100 bill appeared perfect, Burns reasoned, then

it must have been made by the new photoengraving process. But the news story had reported that the printing was sharp and clear to the smallest detail, and photoetching as yet worked only on softer metals that couldn't reproduce such clarity. Only one answer seemed possible: Someone had perfected a method of photoengraving with steel.

Burns put this theory in writing and mailed it to Chief Hazen. But the Chief evidently wasn't impressed with the idea. Instead of being allowed to explore it further, Burns was ordered to join an operative named Matthew F. Griffin in Chicago and check up on a number of old-time engravers there.

None of these suspects had the skill even to approximate such a counterfeit, but for several weeks Burns dutifully carried on an investigation he was certain would lead nowhere. Then early in March of 1898, he was surprised by sudden orders to report to Washington immediately.

The Secret Service had a new Chief — a former editor and star crime reporter for the Chicago *Tribune* named John E. Wilkie. Running across Burns' letter, Wilkie had studied it and agreed that the photoengraving-on-steel theory was the only conceivable answer.

The obvious first move was to compile a list of all engravers who might have evolved such a photoetching method. Burns went directly to Philadelphia where the counterfeit had been discovered. There, with the help of Operative Bill McManus, who was in charge of the territory for the Secret Service, he began making the rounds of local engraving establishments.

Other Secret Service men were doing the same thing throughout the nation. The case was so important that Wilkie himself left the Washington office in the hands of an assistant and personally headed the New York City phase of the investigation.

Personnel records of engraving plants were examined. Operatives also posed as prospective employers. Inserting help-wanted advertisements in local newspapers, they obtained detailed histories of a variety of applicants. Within two weeks, every man in North America capable of doing expert photo-etching was under investigation.

Then, just as this vast operation was reaching its height, Chief Wilkie got a wire from Philadelphia. Burns claimed he had located the guilty engravers.

Burns and McManus had followed the same procedures that were being used everywhere, including the insertion of ads in the Philadelphia *Inquirer*. But Burns had decided to check out local dry goods stores as well. Counterfeiters generally used large amounts of muslin, pressing their paper between wet sheets of it just before printing. At a store on Filbert Street, Burns found a salesman who remembered an unusually big order of muslin bought by a well-dressed young man the autumn before.

"Is there anything else at all you can remember about him?" the detective persisted.

The clerk thought hard. "He kept winking, as if he had something in his eye."

Engravers often get particles of metal or grinding dust in their eyes. A check of the doctors of the area turned up a physician, also on Filbert Street, who could remember a well-dressed young patient with such a complaint. The man had come in on a chill October day, the doctor also recalled, wearing neither a hat nor a topcoat.

The absence of hat and coat, Burns decided, meant that the fellow either lived or worked nearby. Burns and McManus had compiled, by then, a complete list of local photoengravers and found that none lived in the neighborhood. But two men on the list — former employees of the E. A. Wright Company engraving establishment — had recently gone into business for themselves, setting up a printing and engraving shop on the fourth floor of a building at North and Filbert Streets. One was an artistic engraver named

Arthur Taylor, the other a reputed mechanical genius named Baldwin Bredell.

Renting a small office directly across Filbert Street from the new shop, Burns and McManus brought in both the clerk who had sold the muslin and the doctor who had treated the sore eye. Watching with field glasses, both identified Arthur Taylor. It was then that Bill Burns got off his wire to Chief Wilkie.

Wilkie was visibly disappointed when he arrived on the next train from New York. There wasn't one real piece of evidence against the two partners, he pointed out.

Burns had to admit this was true, and he doubted that a raid would produce any evidence. With all the publicity, Bredell and Taylor almost certainly had the plates hidden in some remote spot and were keeping nothing incriminating in their shop. But he was positive they were the men. All the Secret Service could do now, he suggested, was establish an around-the-clock surveillance, sit tight, and wait for the pair to make a suspicious move.

Wilkie commented dryly that it was easy for Burns to talk about sitting tight — he wasn't the one who had the Secretary of the Treasury on his neck. But the Chief could think of no better plan, so he brought in more men to join Burns and McManus, renting rooms that overlooked the residences of both engravers as well as their shop.

Since it seemed likely to Bill Burns that this Philadelphia assignment would last for a while, and since he hadn't seen his family in six months, he wired his wife Annie to join him. Only the baby, Kathleen, could come along because the other children were in school. Burns found rooms in a boarding-house with a small park nearby where his daughter could play on spring afternoons.

By this time, Burns was trying to get a look inside the engraving shop without rousing the suspicions of Bredell and Taylor. The shop door was invariably locked at night. About 3:30 one morning, Burns climbed onto the shoulders of an operative named John Murphy, caught the bottom of a fire escape and started climbing. He'd just reached the fourth floor when he heard a loud voice boom out below:

"What are you doing around here at this hour of the morning?"

Tight to the wall, Burns moved his eyes downward and saw that the newcomer was a policeman.

The Secret Service didn't want its interest in the neighborhood known even to the local police, so Murphy hurridly explained that he couldn't get to sleep and had decided to take a walk. The two men talked for a few minutes and then walked off together. Burns hadn't been spotted, but it had been a close call. There undoubtedly would have been a noisy exchange if he had been discovered, and word might have got back to Bredell and Taylor that they were being watched.

Trying to force a window of the engraving shop, Burns found it locked from the inside. Edging his way precariously along a ledge, he climbed over a coping and tried a second window, but it was locked as well. He gave up then, climbed back to the street and returned to the rented office across the way. Dawn found him eyeing the building thoughtfully. His daytime relief, Assistant Operative Larry Richey, had just arrived when Burns saw a cleaning boy of about thirteen or fourteen arrive at the building. The boy swept and emptied the wastebaskets at several places of business, including the Bredell-Taylor shop.

"He has to have a key," Burns muttered to himself.

When the youngster had finished his work, he suddenly appeared on the fire escape. High on the iron bars above a still-deserted street, he began performing acrobatic tricks.

Richey commented that the boy did this every morning and added that he was almost good enough to go on the stage.

Burns agreed and decided the Secret Service would set up an audition.

The following morning, after the cleaning boy finished

his work, he was stopped on the street by Assistant Operative Richey, who had a large package under his arm.

"Want to make a quick half dollar?" he offered. "Take this bundle over to Mr. Matthews at Guy's Hotel."

"Mr. Matthews?" the boy asked.

"Yes, Matthews, the theatrical agent," Richey told him in a tone that suggested everyone knew who Mr. Matthews was. "Hurry it over there, will you?"

Mr. Matthews was Operative Burns. When the breathless boy arrived and seemed strongly inclined to hang around, Burns unwrapped the bundle in front of him. The young man gasped at the sight of a beautiful velvet costume the Secret Service had rented.

"What do you do nights, son?" Burns suddenly asked.

"Nothing," the boy told him.

Would he be interested, the pseudo theatrical agent wondered, in a walk-on part at the Walnut Street Theatre? The boy was very much interested. Burns explained that the theatre manager was in an adjoining room, and suggested that the young man change into the costume before going in for an interview.

While Operative John Murphy, playing the theatre manager, made the boy strike every pose imaginable and give a detailed account of his life's history as well, Burns was digging into the pockets of the pants that had been shed. Finding a set of keys, he sprinted the six blocks to the Yale Lock Company, where he had prearranged to have duplicates promptly made. He rushed back to replace the keys, then knocked on Murphy's door. The cleaning boy was dismissed with hearty compliments about his acting talent and the stock promise that he'd be notified if anything turned up.

Hopes high, Burns, Murphy and Richey entered the engraving shop that night and spent several hours making a thorough search, testing drawers and files for false bottoms and secret compartments. They found absolutely nothing that could be considered evidence of counterfeiting.

Even so, Burns remained positive that Baldwin Bredell and

Arthur Taylor were the Monroe-head counterfeiters. Though there was no sign of illegal business in their shop, neither was there any sign of legal business. Investigation had shown that the two men discouraged potential customers by asking impossible prices. Yet both were living and dressing extremely well. As early spring gave way to late spring, the shop was searched each night and checked each noon when the partners left for lunch.

One day when Burns was making the noon inspection, he walked past the door of the shop and checked his signals from the fourth floor hall window as usual. Both shades were down in the office the Secret Service had rented, which meant that both Bredell and Taylor had been seen leaving the building and hadn't returned. Burns walked back to the shop and was just reaching for the key in his pocket when the door suddenly opened, and he found himself face to face with Bredell.

"Is this the Eagle Printing Company?" he hurriedly asked.

"No," Bredell told him, "that's on the second floor."

Burns apologized politely, then hurried down and across the street and angrily demanded an explanation from the men who were supposed to be keeping watch for him. They were just as surprised as he was. It turned out that there was another entrance to the engravers' building through a tavern around the corner. Bredell had used it in returning to his shop after an abbreviated lunch. From that time on, both entrances were watched during the noon inspection, with new signals arranged.

Once, when Burns was making the nightly search of the shop, he went through three rooms, started to enter the fourth, then suddenly snapped off his flashlight and dropped to the floor. He'd caught a brief glimpse of a sleeping figure on the cot beside the far wall.

For several minutes, he debated what to do next. If Bredell or Taylor or whoever was on that cot was really asleep, Burns knew he could slip silently back out. But suppose the man had heard him enter and was only feigning sleep? In that case, the Secret Service would have to make an immediate raid and hope that the still-missing evidence could be turned up later.

Burns decided he couldn't leave without being sure the unmoving figure was actually sleeping. Creeping inch by inch across the floor, he stared ahead by the faint moonlight that filtered in through the window. When he was beside the cot at last, he found something that he didn't report to Chief Wilkie or anyone else for quite a few years — an old overcoat and a wadded white cleaning rag that in the dimness and the brief sweep of his flashlight bore a startling resemblance to an upturned human face.

More weeks passed. Burns' older son, George, just sixteen, had run off to join the army, hoping to get into the Spanish-American War. Annie and Kathleen rushed back to Ohio, the authorities were contacted and the adventurous boy was returned home for being underage. Meantime, Bill Burns in Philadelphia continued the steady searching of the engraving shop and the shadowing of its owners. He still turned up nothing. Secretary of the Treasury Gage had lost patience, and Secret Service Chief Wilkie was trying to decide between making arrests without real evidence or dropping the surveillance entirely when the two suspected engravers suddenly left Philadelphia. They enjoyed themselves for a time at Atlantic City and then sailed off on a European vacation.

A number of the counterfeit $100 Monroe-head bills turned up in Atlantic City. And several people who'd received them identified photos of Bredell and Taylor as the passers.

This gave the Secret Service a doubtful case at best. Defense lawyers often won acquittals for bill passers, simply by reminding jurors that they, too, could unknowingly pass counterfeit currency some day. But there was no longer any doubt among Burns' superiors that he had located the right engravers. The detective took advantage of the partners' European vacation to spend some time with his family in

Sir Arthur Conan Doyle with Burns family

Burns at demonstration of bulletproof vest in Washington, D.C., 1923

Columbus. But he was back in Philadelphia when Bredell and Taylor returned in early autumn and supervised again the watching of their every move.

The case was now almost a year old, and something seemed to be stirring. Fresh materials were found on the noon and midnight searches of the shop, suggesting the engravers were starting a new piece of work. One morning Bredell and Taylor left the Filbert Street building, walked to the Broad Street railroad station and caught a train for Lancaster, Pennsylvania. Operative Mat Griffin, brought in from Chicago to help with the Philadelphia operation, followed the pair that morning.

In Lancaster, the two partners contacted a cigar-factory owner named William Jacobs and a man named William Kendig, who owned a nearby tobacco warehouse. Upon hearing of this, Chief Wilkie obtained a supply of the cigars that Jacobs manufactured and had the blue revenue stamps on the boxes examined closely.

A case that was already the biggest in Secret Service history became even bigger. The stamps were counterfeit, made from skillful photoengravings, and they seemed to be the work of the same craftsmen who'd turned out the Monroe-head bill.

Treasury Secretary Gage wanted Jacobs and Kendig arrested immediately, but there was still no evidence against Bredell and Taylor that would hold up in court. Wilkie pleaded for delay, arguing that an arrest would tip off the two engravers and waste a surveillance of many months. Gage finally agreed. Additional operatives were rushed to Pennsylvania in such numbers that several districts were stripped to skeleton forces that could do little more than man the offices.

Burns reasoned that if the counterfeiters were doing their printing in Lancaster, they were almost certainly using Kendig's often-deserted warehouse for this purpose, rather than the busy cigar factory. Once again he had the problem of getting in to search without giving the owner any reason for suspicion.

The three-story warehouse had a big main door with an inside spring latch and a small side door with a glass window. Kendig always latched the front door from the outside, then left by the side door — locking it during the day and at night adding heavy shutters that were locked as well.

Burns borrowed a small boy from his roominghouse neighborhood in Philadelphia, telling him that he wanted to play a joke on a friend. Rehearsing the boy carefully, he treated the youngster to a crisp five-dollar bill, a new baseball and a train ride to Lancaster. When Kendig left the warehouse at noon that day, Burns promptly smashed the side window, tossed the ball inside, then lifted the boy carefully through and told him to unlatch the main door. While other operatives kept a careful watch, Burns swiftly searched the building.

On the second floor, he found a large quantity of the blue paper the government used for printing tobacco revenue stamps. It looked genuine, and he suspected it was stolen. He also discovered that a corner of the third floor had recently been partitioned off and was tightly bolted and padlocked. This seemed a likely place for counterfeiters to keep a printing press.

Hurrying downstairs, Burns showed his young helper how to relatch the front door. Then Burns went outside and around to the locked side door where he lifted the boy carefully back out through the shattered window.

When warehouse owner Kendig got back from lunch, he had cigar manufacturer Jacobs with him. They found a small boy waiting tearfully.

"Can I have my ball back?" he begged, as he'd been coached to do. "My dad'll pay for the window."

Men who manufacture their own money can afford to be generous. Jacobs and Kendig retrieved the baseball, patted the youngster's shoulder and told him to forget about the window.

By the end of 1898, the long, large-scale stake out had

produced enough evidence for U. S. District Attorney James Beck of Philadelphia to be certain that he could convict Kendig and Jacobs as well as a Deputy of Internal Revenue named Samual Downey, whom they had bribed to help them, and Kendig's warehouse foreman — a fellow named, to Bill Burns' embarrassment, James Burns.

But no arrests were made. The most wanted men of the entire counterfeiting ring, Baldwin Bredell and Arthur Taylor, were still implicated only by association and sketchy circumstantial evidence. Even though they had been watched constantly for nearly a year, they had yet to give themselves away. Bill Burns was hopeful that a long-awaited break was coming when on February 11, 1899, he shadowed Kendig and Jacobs to the train station in Lancaster and discovered they were setting out for Philadelphia. He expected them to go to the Bredell-Taylor shop in the Filbert Street building and perhaps initiate some new activity in the course of which the two wary engravers finally would betray themselves. But Kendig and Jacobs called instead at the office of two of Pennsylvania's most reputable attorneys — Ellery P. Ingham, a former U. S. District Attorney who had preceded Beck in the post at Philadelphia, and his former assistant and current partner, Harvey K. Newitt.

Being visited by counterfeiters was, in itself, nothing to cast suspicion on a pair of highly respected lawyers. But that very afternoon, Newitt surreptitiously took Operative Bill McManus aside while McManus was waiting to give a report to District Attorney Beck.

"There was a man in my office today," Newitt mentioned softly, "with $1500 to spend for something in your office — $500 for myself and $1,000 to spend as I see fit."

McManus didn't yet know about the visit of the two Lancaster men to the firm of Ingham and Newitt. "There's nothing in my office worth $1,000," he said.

"Well, let's put it this way," the lawyer continued. "I have a client who is willing to pay $1,500 a month to make sure that any mention of him that comes into your office doesn't get out of your office." (Actually, the two Philadelphia lawyers had blandly told the Lancaster tobacco men that it would cost $3,000 a month to buy off the Secret Service; they intended keeping $2,000 for themselves.)

McManus agreed to consider the offer, then promptly reported it to Chief Wilkie. When Burns reported that Kendig and Jacobs had been in touch with Newitt, it became obvious that the pair from Lancaster somehow had begun to suspect they were being watched. Most likely, Wilkie reasoned, Deputy Internal Revenue Collector Downey had gotten wind of the investigation. Even the Secret Service couldn't keep a surveillance of this size secret forever.

Ordinarily, such suspicion on the part of men under observation calls for immediate raids and arrests to prevent the destruction of evidence. But if Kendig and Jacobs could be led to believe the Secret Service was being bought off, the watching game could go on a little longer, in the hope of getting a case against engravers Bredell and Taylor. McManus was told to let the lawyer bribe him. When no further approach had been made by March 6, he went directly to Newitt's office and said that he was willing to accept the deal.

Newitt nodded, but seemed extremely nervous at having a Secret Service man openly calling on him.

"Do you have the money?" McManus demanded bluntly, as he later reported the encounter.

"Not yet, but I will," Newitt assured him. "This man is responsible." Then Newitt became evasive. "Does your district include Lancaster?" he asked.

"Yes."

"What are you working on right now?"

"Government pension frauds," McManus told him.

"What's Burns doing around this district, then?"

"The same thing."

Newitt seemed skeptical. "He's a nosey devil. I've seen him hanging around this very building."

McManus shrugged. "There are a lot of offices in this building. Burns is just helping me. This district is in my charge entirely."

Newitt looked satisfied. "Then you can give me full assurance that if I pay you certain persons will be secure for one month?"

The Secret Service man nodded.

"Meet me at the Lafayette Hotel tomorrow then. Don't come to the office again."

When McManus kept that appointment, it was obvious that Newitt had decided to try for an even bigger cut of the protection money. The lawyer handed McManus only $500, saying that was all he had.

Deciding that a real bribe taker wouldn't stand still for this, McManus accepted the roll of bills but warned Newitt to come up with another like it soon. On March 28, the attorney reluctantly gave him another $500 — to be marked and turned over to Chief Wilkie as the first payment had been.

The Secret Service surveillance had been expanded to include the two lawyers by then, making a total of eight men whose homes, places of work and every movement were being watched around the clock. Burns was back spending all of his time at the all-important Filbert Street stake out, realizing in desperation that unless evidence against the engraving-shop partners was obtained soon, the arrests would have to be made without them. In mid-April, he found what he needed.

There was a small locker in one of the rooms he was regularly searching that he invariably found unlocked and empty at night. Yet at noon, of late, it was always locked securely. This suggested the engravers had begun working on something they didn't dare leave in their shop overnight. Burns spent most of one night cutting key blanks to shape by trial and error until he had one that would fit the locker. He slipped in at noon the next day, opened it, and found a partially completed plate for a new $100 bill.

The raids and arrests began on April 18, a year and a half after the first bogus Monroe-head silver certificate had been detected and a full year after Burns had first identified

Taylor and Bredell as the men he suspected. The Secret Service had twenty men in Philadelphia and a dozen more waiting in Lancaster. Elaborate precautions were taken. Accompanied by Operative John Murphy, Burns slipped into the engraving shop, identified himself to Arthur Taylor when he returned from lunch and handcuffed him. Bredell arrived a few minutes later. Both men were shown the warrants for their arrests. Then Chief Wilkie and a dozen other Secret Service men came crowding into the shop. The locker was opened in the prisoners' presence and the unfinished new plates lifted out, these with a head of Lincoln instead of Monroe.

"Where are the others?" Burns demanded crisply.

Before Bredell could stop him, Taylor blurted out that they were hidden in the home of Bredell's family in Camden, New Jersey, under some foundation stones just to the left of the front cellar window. Bredell countered by mentioning that a numbering machine used on the counterfeit bills was hidden in Taylor's family home in Philadelphia. Before long, these two men — both gifted and well-educated, and neither of whom had ever previously been in trouble with the law — were talking rapidly and revealing the entire story. They had been approached early in 1896 and offered $25,000 to make counterfeit revenue stamps for Jacobs and Kendig. Using their photoengraving process, they'd gone on to the counterfeiting of actual currency the following year.

"One thing still puzzles me," Burns admitted during the process of getting signed statements from the pair. "Where did you get the blue paper for those revenue stamps with a U.S.I.R. (United States Internal Revenue) watermark on it? It looks genuine, but there's no record of any theft of government paper."

"Kendig tore a corner off a real revenue stamp, then took it up to an old paper-mill owner at Chambersburg," Taylor explained.

"He told the man he wanted the same color and type of

paper for a patent medicine label, and he wanted it water-marked with the initials — Uncle Sam's Indian Remedy." Burns slumped in a chair and laughed almost uncontrollably.

Leaving Bredell and Taylor under guard at Philadelphia, Wilkie and Burns caught the next train for Lancaster, where a platoon of operatives awaited them. They spent a sleepless night in the tobacco warehouse. At about 6:30 A.M., fore-man James Burns arrived. As he was being arrested he went after Operative Burns with ham-sized fists swinging. Other operatives overpowered and handcuffed him.

In contrast, when warehouse owner Kendig showed up, he reacted to arrest by promising over and over again, "I'll make no trouble." Then Burns and Operative Schuyler Donella went to the cigar factory, to locate William Jacobs. Jacobs gasped when he saw an arrest warrant and ordered a clerk who was present to leave the office.

"Let him stay," Donella shrugged. "He'll know about it soon enough anyway."

"Don't be foolish," Jacobs whispered. After waving the clerk from the room, he opened a wall safe and counted out $14,000 in genuine currency, stacking it on his desk. "I think you gentlemen made a mistake, didn't you?" he smiled hopefully.

The two operatives shook their heads.

"Give me just ten minutes," Jacobs pleaded. "I can double it at least, and maybe even get more. I thought you . . . "

"You thought we'd already been taken care of? For just the $1,500 you gave Ingham and Newitt? You must think we come cheap."

"Why, those crooks" Jacobs exploded. "I've been paying them $3,000 a month" Before his rage subsided, he signed a full, written confession.

When Burns returned to the warehouse, he found Kendig still declining to make a statement but plaintively protesting the handcuffs on his wrists. "Please don't make me wear them outside," he begged. "I won't make any trouble. But I've never known disgrace like this before. If my father saw me, it would kill him."

"If you feel bad about him now," Burns said, tonelessly and pitilessly, "you'll feel a lot worse when we arrest him."

Kendig was hysterical. "What for?"

"Because he hid those plates for the revenue stamps for you," Burns bluffed.

"No, he didn't. He didn't even know about them," Kendig sobbed. And by way of proving it, he led the Secret Service men to the top floor of the warehouse and showed them a loose brick in the wall. Behind it lay not only the revenue stamp plates but also the long-sought plates for the $100 Monroe-head bill that had set off the vast investigation.

"Then what plates were Bredell and Taylor talking about?" Wilkie and Burns both wondered aloud. Not until other operatives returned from Camden, New Jersey, did the Secret Service learn that the engravers had blundered into revealing a set of plates for a $50 bill which none of the investigators had known existed.

The lengthy large-scale operation could be made public at last. Chief John Wilkie described it to reporters as "the most important capture in the history of the Secret Service." He then identified William J. Burns as the operative "by whose efforts the unearthing of the counterfeit conspiracy was largely accomplished." When Wilkie went into some of the details, veteran newsmen shook their heads in amazement.

"Sounds like Sherlock Holmes' work," Edward Marshall of *The New York Times* said.

"No, just Billy Burns' work," Wilkie said, with a proud smile. "He was picked especially for this job." Wilkie then reviewed how Burns had suspected the counterfeiters were using a new photoengraving process, and had been brought to Philadelphia from Chicago to follow his hunch. "In just two weeks," Wilkie continued, "Burns knew who the engravers were, even though it took us more than a year to dig up all the facts and bring the case to a successful conclusion. It was a brilliant piece of work."

A $27,000,000 currency issue had been made secure. A revenue stamp fraud that had cost the government $250,000 a year had been exposed. And counterfeit plates that could have cost an inestimable additional amount had been captured before they were used. On April 22, 1899, Bill Burns was rewarded with the highest pay rate permissable for an operative — seven dollars a day.

On his next visit with his family, he dressed them all in their Sunday best, from three-year-old Kathleen up to 17-year-old George, and made a formal occasion out of parading down to the Columbus Savings and Loan Building. There, he and Annie drew out everything she'd managed to put away dollar by dollar and made a down payment on a new house over on Wilson Street. After eighteen years of marriage, they finally owned a home of their own.

Disposition of the Monroe-head case seemed routine in that spring of 1899. With the exception of the two bribe-offering lawyers, all of the arrested persons waived preliminary hearings and made it clear they intended pleading guilty, hoping for the best as first offenders. By May 17, U.S. District Attorney James Beck had obtained indictments of all involved.

Burns was back working out of the New York office that summer, remaining in readiness to testify and handling only minor assignments that could be interrupted on short notice. Reporting daily to the federal building that contained the Secret Service office, he found himself being befriended by a young government clerk.

This was not unusual in itself. He was well-known now and the center of a great deal of attention. His zest for story telling and his unreformed theatrical leanings also made him a widely-sought luncheon companion. But after several such invitations, he sensed that this particular clerk wanted more than the pleasure of his company. Something was obviously troubling the man and troubling him deeply.

Burns finally forced the point. "You've been just about to tell me something any number of times. What is it?"

"I'm being blackmailed," the young man finally blurted out. "At least I think I am."

After pledging Burns to secrecy, the clerk told his story. Years before, he'd made a cross-country bicycle trip with a friend. On a lark, during the trip, they got into trouble. Both served brief jail sentences, but by giving false names and addresses to the local police, they'd managed to keep the experience a secret. Later on, when the young man had filled out an application for his government job, he had lied about the arrest in fear of being disqualified.

He had a faultless employment record. He had been commended by his superiors and promoted regularly. He'd almost forgotten the fact that he had falsified his application. Then his old bicycle-trip companion had showed up in New York a few months ago, opening a small watch-repair shop just a few blocks away.

"When I first met him again," the young man explained, "it seemed perfectly natural for him to talk about that time we went to jail together. But he kept coming around and every time we saw each other he mentioned the subject. Then he asked me to lend him $300 to help get his shop started. He didn't really threaten me. But I didn't dare refuse him."

"And he hasn't repaid you," said Burns rhetorically, "or offered to sign a note?"

The clerk shook his head. "That $300 was just the beginning. He went right on borrowing from me. He kept it all on a friendly basis, and maybe he's not legally guilty of blackmail or anything else. I don't know. Each time he comes around he talks about that summer we were arrested together. Then he asks me for another loan. And I've been afraid to say no."

"How much have you given him altogether?"

"Twenty-seven hundred dollars."

Burns whistled softly.

"It's all I had — years of savings. Now I don't have any more to give him. What do you think he'll do?"

Burns shrugged. "Give me the address of his shop. I'll take care of it."

"How?" the clerk wondered.

"I don't really know yet," Burns explained. "I'll have to size the fellow up."

He did his sizing up that afternoon. He paid a visit to the blackmailing watchmaker to discuss an imaginary fault with his pocket timeplace. When he finally decided on a course of action, he flashed his Secret Service credentials.

"I want some information about a friend of yours." He named the young clerk. "Has he been spending a lot of money? More than he should be spending on his salary? Buying expensive things or gambling perhaps?"

The watch-repairman was speechless for a moment. "Why ask me?"

"Come now" Burns snapped impatiently. "He's been shadowed constantly, and he's been seen with you on several occasions. Now I'll ask you once again, and if I don't get a straight answer I'll take you in. Has he been spending a lot of money lately?"

"Not that I know of," the startled man insisted in honest bewilderment. "Why is he being shadowed? Is he in some sort of trouble?"

"That's not your concern. I'm going to leave the address of my office with you. If you notice him spending more than he ought to be, you'd better notify us immediately. And I warn you — if you say one word to him about this visit, I'll arrest you for obstructing an investigation."

He turned and stalked out, ignoring the puzzled shop owner's further questions. Back at the federal building, he saw the young clerk again.

"What happened?"

"You go see your old friend this evening," Burns told him, "and tell him you're in serious trouble. Tell him the government is checking up on you because there's a shortage of . . . say $3500 in your accounts. Tell him he got $2700 of it, and you took the other $800 and gambled it away trying to make up and replace what you'd given him."

The clerk gradually began to see Burns' plan. "What if he says it's strictly my problem?" he wondered. "That it hasn't anything to do with him?"

"That's almost certainly what he'll say. And he'll probably warn you to keep his name out of it and threaten you by mentioning the time you were arrested. But tell him you know the government investigators will demand to know what you did with the money, that you're afraid they'll keep after you until you tell the whole story. Of course, you can make it clear that you're no longer worried about having an old arrest record revealed. At most, that would mean losing your job. Embezzling will mean years in prison."

"But even if it were true," the clerk asked, "would he really be guilty of anything more than borrowing money from an embezzler?"

"*He* knows he hasn't just been borrowing money. He'll *feel* guilty of being a party to embezzlement as well as blackmail now. At the very least, this should stop him from asking for any more loans, and there's a good chance he'll come up with as much of the money he's taken from you as he possibly can."

The clerk was still skeptical, but he agreed to do as he was told. Burns had to leave for Philadelphia the next day and confer with federal district attorney Beck about the forthcoming trial of the counterfeiters. A chance for a visit to Columbus followed. Altogether, nearly two weeks passed before he returned to New York, but he hadn't forgotten his spare-time blackmail case. Curious as to what results his scheme had produced, he caught the clerk at lunch hour his first day back.

76

"He came up with the whole thing," the young fellow said incredulously.

"The whole $2700?" Burns was amazed himself.

The clerk shook his head. "The whole *$3500*! Either he didn't really need money all that time, or he mortgaged his shop or something. But that's what he gave me."

Over lunch, Burns listened eagerly to the details — how the watch-repairman had blustered and threatened, how he'd sworn for days that he didn't have a cent with which to help.

"Didn't he try to get you to settle for less?" Burns asked.

The clerk nodded. "But once I'd told him it was $3500 I'd stolen I couldn't very well change my story, could I? Now I owe him $800. What should I do?"

Burns laughed so heartily everyone in the place turned to stare at him. "Tell your old friend that you're very grateful and that you'll pay him back out of your salary, that you can afford to give him . . . say $10 a month for the next 80 months. I don't think he'll be blackmailing you again."

On October 10, 1899, the Philadelphia-Lancaster counterfeiters finally were brought to trial. As expected, all pleaded guilty except Ingham and Newitt, the two attorneys charged with attempted bribery. They both swore they'd been framed by the Secret Service, but they too were convicted after an 11-day trial during which the Secret Service had to arrest three more men for attempting to bribe the jury.

With his testimony given, Burns went on to other assignments — including his celebrated tracking down of the anonymous note writer who had threatened the life of British Ambassador Julian Pauncefote. On November 25, sentences of various lengths were given to all involved in the Pennsylvania counterfeiting conspiracy. Having thrown themselves on the mercy of the court, engraving partners Arthur Taylor and Baldwin Bredell found the court none too merciful. Both received twelve years in prison. And this sentence laid the groundwork for a weird and puzzling aftermath to what had appeared a fully resolved case.

It began when Burns was called to Washington by Chief Wilkie and handed a newly-discovered counterfeit $20 bill to examine.

"What do you think of it?" Wilkie asked.

"It's a good one."

"Who do you think could have made it?"

"It is the handiwork of Baldwin Bredell and Arthur Taylor!"

"Impossible!" Wilkie replied. He went on to point out what they already knew: that he and Burns had both been certain that all the plates had been found in the Monroehead case, including the set the Secret Service hadn't known existed; and that except for being led to and from court in handcuffs, Bredell and Taylor hadn't been out of their cell in Moyamensing Penitentiary since then.

Burns couldn't argue with any of this. He was as positive as his chief that the two cell mates had told everything at the time of their arrest. But every expert photo engraver had been thoroughly checked out a year ago. The process of elimination had led to Bredell and Taylor then. And it still did, as impossible as it seemed.

Burns decided to gamble on a direct confrontation. Calling at Moyamensing, he sent for Bredell and Taylor and showed them the bill.

"Here's a new note that turned up."

"It's a beauty" Bredell exclaimed.

"Who made it?" Taylor piped up.

Neither voice rang true. Nor did the looks on their faces.

"You did," Burns told them.

The two men were curiously half hearted in denying the charge. After surprisingly little persistence on Burns' part, they smilingly explained that they'd had a set of $20 plates hidden at the time of their arrest.

"Now you want to make a deal, I suppose?" Burns asked. "You want me to see Jim Beck and try to get those 12-year sentences reduced in return for the plates that printed this bill?"

The two engravers agreed, rather smugly, that this thought was certainly worth discussing.

Burns stared at them a moment, then chuckled softly. "I guess you've got us. And I think I even know where you picked up the idea. There was an article on Long Bill Brockway in a Sunday newspaper a few years back, and it told how he escaped prison a half-dozen times — by keeping one set of plates hidden and using them to bargain for his freedom if he got caught — right up until we landed him for good in 1895."

Bredell and Taylor allowed that they just might have read such an article. Then they suggested that plates as perfect as the ones they had hidden should be worth a good many years off their sentences. Otherwise, they threatened, the Secret Service would see a flood of those $20 bills."

"I'll see what Beck says," Burns agreed. But instead, he went directly back to Washington to see what Chief Wilkie would say — reporting that Bredell and Taylor had admitted making the plates.

"When did they make them?" Wilkie wondered.

"Before their arrest, they say. But they're lying." Burns went on to explain that he felt the prisoners had "over-trained" themselves, that they'd practiced their story too often, that it sounded too pat, too perfect. Then he mentioned the newspaper story about Brockway. "It wasn't printed a couple of years ago. It appeared less than two months ago."

"Bill," the Chief asked, "are you trying to tell me that those two photoengraved a pair of plates in prison?"

Burns nodded.

"How?"

"I don't know how."

"It can't be. They were just agreeing with anything you

said when you mentioned that article about Brockway. They must have had the $20 plates hidden when we raided their shop."

"I'm positive they didn't," Burns argued stubbornly.

Wilkie wanted to talk with the prisoners themselves. He and Burns went to Philadelphia, picked up U.S. District Attorney Beck, and called at the prison. After hearing Bredell and Taylor tell their story, both Wilkie and Beck came away convinced that the only thing left to do was make a deal for the plates. And both agreed that, wherever the photo engraving had been done, it hadn't been done in a Moyamensing cell. The inmates were under constant watch in the daytime, they argued, and checked regularly by flashlight-carrying guards through the night.

The point was important. For plates made before their arrest, Bredell and Taylor could make whatever demands they wished with no fear of further punishment. But if they had actually found a way to make photoengraved plates in a prison cell, and it could be proven that they had done this, the threat of stiff, additional second-offense sentences could be held over their heads.

Burns adamantly continued to oppose a deal. Out of respect for his past record of uninterrupted success, Wilkie and Beck finally consented to hold up any offer of reduced sentences until he had a chance to investigate further. Burns then went back to Moyamensing alone.

Waiting until Bredell and Taylor were out in the yard for an exercise period, he inspected the cell they occupied. He didn't discover any counterfeiting apparatus, but he did find that the cell contained a small alcove and that there were marks on the sides and tops that might well have been made by the hanging of a curtain.

Flipping through the prison register, Burns next learned that the pair had been visited regularly by a Philadelphia lawyer of shady reputation, and by Arthur Taylor's brother and widowed mother. When Burns checked the visitors' room he saw that the surveillance was lax enough so that small items might be slipped through the gratings to the prisoners.

It was true that counterfeiting by the photoengraving method involved heavy, bulky equipment. It was also true, though, Burns reminded himself, that Baldwin Bredell was a mechanical genius and conceivably might have figured out a way to do the work with smaller gear.

Alone in a hotel room that night, Burns tried to reconstruct what might have happened. Screened by a blanket, the alcove could have served as both a secret working place and a darkroom. A dummy, made up of clothes in a bunk, could have fooled the guards while one man was secretly working at night. Tools and plates could have been smuggled in, as well as small amounts of the needed chemicals and supplies. Setting up a press in the cell seemed totally impossible, but the actual printing could well have been done by a confederate after the completed plates had been smuggled outside.

Even so, there was one problem that still seemed insurmountable. To photoengrave the counterfeit plates, a picture had to be taken of a genuine $20 bill. And to do this properly, with the process of photoetching on steel that Taylor had perfected, took far more skill than any outside confederate could very likely have possessed. How had the prisoners managed to get and use a camera?

Even Bredell couldn't have constructed one with the necessary settings and focus from disassembled parts received through the gratings. And what kind of camera could have taken the needed picture by the light of the candle or small lamp the prisoners must have used?

Dawn was coming into the sky beyond the hotel room window when Burns suddenly remembered that he'd once built a camera of sorts himself, following instructions in a book he'd had as a boy. It had been a crude affair called a "pinhole" camera, little more than a light-tight box with a tiny hole in front instead of a lens. But when clamped

81

perfectly still in front of a stationary object for a long enough time, it had taken vividly clear pictures. Had Bredell also remembered this novelty of an earlier era and perhaps improved upon the pinhole principle?

Burns didn't know. But he knew as much as he would ever know unless the prisoners themselves told him more. Returning to Moyamensing, he asked to Arthur Taylor alone.

Taylor wondered if there had been any word about a deal for the plates.

Of course not, Burns snorted contemptuously. Did they really think they convinced anyone they'd made the plates prior to their arrest? Wilkie and Beck knew as well as he, Burns asserted, exactly where and when and how they were made. Nobody in authority had ever seriously considered a reduction in the prisoners' sentences, he went on. The only question now was the size of the new sentences they would get for this second offense — at least 20 years if they persisted in their denials.

"Taylor," he pointed out grimly, "you are going to be here in prison for the rest of your life."

Taylor seemed shaken. But he caught himself and began arguing that Burns' accusation was impossible, that no one could do photoengraving in a Moyamensing cell.

That might be true, the Secret Service man answered, if the security in the visiting room were a little tighter and the openings in the gratings a little smaller, and if some of the cells weren't conveniently equipped with alcoves. Mentioning as much else as he'd guessed, and strongly suggesting that he knew all the rest, he waved his hand as though refusing to discuss things both of them knew any longer. "What I can't understand," he admitted "is why you let Bredell make such a dope of you."

Taylor demanded to know what he meant.

"Was it Bredell's brother who made himself an accessory? Was it *his* widowed mother who'll probably go to prison now for trying to help her son?"

82

Arthur Taylor was silent for a long time. If the Secret Service got the plates, he finally asked, would his mother be left alone?

The plates and a full confession, Burns countered.

How much of an added sentence would that mean?

A short one, or possibly none, if they cooperated all the way.

"Let me have a half hour with Bredell," Taylor asked at last.

At the end of that half hour, the two prisoners sent for Bill Burns, told their entire story and signed statements. They had spent about two months working in their improvised darkroom. And to Burns' surprise, they had done the printing there as well as the photoengraving — bleaching dollar bills for paper and running them through a tiny press Bredell had rigged up. Henry Taylor, Arthur's brother, had passed about 45 of the counterfeit twenties, destroying the rest as soon as he was certain the Secret Service knew of the bills.

The prisoners hadn't been trying to profit by their prison-made plates; they had wanted only to trade them for a reduction of their sentences. All of the equipment had been smuggled back out the moment the job was done. Along with the plates, it was buried, of all places, in the grave of Taylor's father.

Burns took the still-skeptical Chief Wilkie with him when they dug up the grave; and on May 9, 1900, Henry Taylor was found in New York and arrested. With the signed statements, the strange case seemed headed for routine conclusion.

But Bredell and Taylor made the mistake of talking to their lawyer again. They decided to repudiate their confessions and stand trial. And when that trial began, they had the full backing of the Moyamensing Penitentiary authorities, who were furious at being made the laughingstock of the newspapers and vehemently argued that the counterfeiting could not have been done in one of their cells.

The defense brought in a photography expert who testified that it would be impossible to take the needed picture by lamplight or candlelight with any known make of camera. But after he spent hours on an involved explanation of lenses and apertures and shutter speeds, a simple demonstration with a pinhole camera demolished his testimony.

An expert printer testified that the press which had produced the counterfeit bills entered in evidence must have weighed at least eighty pounds. Bill Burns took the miniscule press he'd found in the grave from his coat pocket — a cunningly designed affair made from sections of washing-machine rollers — and the witness could only stare in amazement as it was demonstrated.

The jury said guilty. Baldwin Bredell and Arthur Taylor ended up with seven years added to their original sentences.

On August 21, James M. Beck, now an assistant Attorney General, got off a letter to William J. Burns. Noting that the Philadelphia-Lancaster matter was finally closed and that the fate of the last of the counterfeiters was finally determined, Beck wished to "take this occasion, as the prosecuting attorney who prosecuted all of these cases, to express not only my great sense of obligation to you for your invaluable cooperation but also my admiration for the unwearying industry, the superb courage, the profound insight, which you displayed from the beginning to the end of this important investigation."

It was in concluding this letter that the admiring official pulled out all the stops and insisted that Sherlock Holmes could have done no better, though he had the advantage of fiction.

The Burns name was such that son George, although just 18, was readily accepted by the Secret Service in that summer of 1900 and assigned to the coveted New York District office. And on July 9, 1901, when Chief Wilkie received a startling wire from the San Francisco office, it could only be Bill Burns whom he put aboard a train and had heading westward within a few hours.

THIRTY THOUSAND DOLLAR SHORTAGE DISCOVERED AT THE MINT, the telegram read. REQUEST ABLEST TALENT IN THE SERVICE.

In a sense, it was the prison-cell counterfeiting case all over again. Once more, the impossible seemed to have happened.

Burns was far from displeased with the sudden assignment. For one thing, a weeks-old heat wave was hanging over the Eastern seaboard. For another, he hadn't had a case that could be described as anything more than routine for fully a year. Whatever the robbery of a United States Mint might be, it certainly wasn't routine.

Since Burns had never before been to San Francisco, he had never seen the money factory that had been so mysteriously plundered. But he knew something of the way mints were guarded, and of the system of checks and balances set up in their bookkeeping.

United States Mints were as nearly robbery- and embezzlement-proof as human ingenuity could make them. Each mint was a business operation that purchased precious metals as raw materials, then turned out coins as a product. Separate sets of books were kept on the weights of metals, the cost of metals, and the face value of coins — with each of these intricate and interdependent accounting systems serving as a check on the others.

Furthermore, the several different departments had daily, weekly, quarterly and annual reports which were sent to Washington individually. And once a year, two expert auditors arrived to check out everything. Juggling the books of a mint was practically a mathematical impossibility.

Moreover, the security system at a mint made any bank seem unguarded by comparison. Windows and doors were covered by a vast system of electric alarms. Night-shift guards were allowed to enter certain areas only in pairs, and these teams of two were reassigned each evening in a patternless manner. Each of the major vaults had a time lock that permitted it to be opened only during working hours, a guard whose sole assignment was to sit staring at its door during those hours, and a combination lock with the combination known to just one high mint official.

Yet somehow, assuming the information in the telegram to be correct, $30,000 was missing from the San Francisco Mint.

Operative Thomas B. Foster met Bill Burns at the station and filled him in on the details. The shortage of six heavy bags of $20 "Double Eagle" gold pieces had been discovered on July 3 in a huge vault located in the office of Cashier Harold Colton, who had been sick at home that day. Only Colton had known the combination to the vault, which was further protected by the night time lock. A copy of the vault combination, however, had been kept in a sealed envelope in the office safe of Mint Superintendent Frank Leach. With Colton absent, the superintendent had slit open his envelope, taken his cashier's place for the day, and discovered the shortage. Operative Foster had carefully examined that envelope. He was positive that it hadn't been tampered with previously.

Would the normal procedure, Burns wondered, have been for Cashier Colton to have the combination changed when he returned to work, sealing up a new copy to leave with the Superintendent?

Foster nodded. As the only man who could have opened the vault alone, everything pointed to Harold Colton. But the Secret Service could hardly arrest the cashier, then try to convince a judge and jury that he must have stolen the gold simply because no one else could have done so. By all appearances, Colton couldn't have done it either.

The time lock on the vault had been tested and found

to be working. How could 1500 gold pieces be carried out, during working hours, under the nose of a full-time watching guard, past dozens of employees and two more guards at the main door?

The shortage seemed so incredible that Superintendent Leach, certain there had to be some mistake, had waited six days, checking and double-checking the records and inventory, before even reporting the matter to the local Secret Service office.

To Burns' mind, wondering who had taken the Double Eagles seemed purposeless at the moment. The first thing he had to figure out was how it could have been done.

He began by visiting the mint, just as anyone might, without identifying himself. Stepping down from a street car, he found himself facing a huge square building of granite with a long flight of stairs that led up to a main door sided by massive columns. Beyond that door, a wide corridor stretched ahead to form the stem of a "T" with another corridor that ran the entire width of the building.

The mint covered a full city block and yet essentially contained but six rooms — a fact that made the theft seem even more fantastic. There were no back passageways or secluded private offices, no small rooms except for the vaults themselves. Openness was the very theme of the place, and for obvious reasons. Each of the more than 200 employees, from the lowest-paid janitor to the superintendent himself, worked within sight of numerous others.

To the right, just beyond the big main door, was a large museum where coins and metals were on public display. To the left, with a single large door opening onto the entrance corridor, was the department headed by Chief Clerk Walter Dimmick. Still farther to the left, reached either through Dimmick's department or through a door on the long transverse corridor, was the office of Superintendent Leach. This made up the front half of the building.

The rear half, beyond the transverse corridor, was walled

off into three sections, all with interconnecting doors and doors opening onto the corridor. From left to right was a receiving room, a weighing room, and the department headed by Cashier Harold Colton, where the plundered vault was located. The main door to that department was at the meeting point of the two corridors, easily seen from any point on either and in plain sight of the guards at the outside entrance.

Burns shook his head slowly, made a small notebook sketch of the floor plan, then identified himself to the head of the security force and asked a few questions.

How was the cashier's vault guarded? he wondered.

The answer was exactly what he'd expected: one man did nothing but watch the door of the vault during daytime working hours; at night, a roving team of two men checked it every 20 minutes.

How many guards were on duty?

Seventeen in the daytime and twelve at night, eight outside and four inside. Some had assigned stations. Others had rounds to make and various bells to ring upon the completion of those rounds.

What security precautions were taken at the entrance?

Any package that came out of the mint was inspected, whether in the hands of a visitor or an employee, including the superintendent. The guards were highly trained men, skilled at spotting even small suspicious bulges in clothing. In fact, the head of the security force still refused to believe that $30,000 in gold could have been stolen from the building. In spite of the thorough 6-day audit Superintendent Leach had ordered, the guards were still certain there was an accounting error somewhere.

Burns was invited, by way of a demonstration of security measures, to watch the precautions that were taken when freshly-minted coins were stored in the very vault where the shortage had been discovered. He saw how the bags of money were wheeled in on a guarded hand-truck, how they were counted separately by three people, then weighed as a cross-check before being sealed and receipted. He was duly impressed. After tracing every possible route from the vault to an outside door, he left the building shaking his head.

"No one took six bags of gold coins from that vault during working hours," he stated flatly when he arrived back at the Secret Service office.

Tom Foster didn't disagree. The San Francisco operative simply reminded Burns that the theft couldn't have been committed at night, either. The time lock was working.

"There must be some way the lock can be put temporarily out of order," Burns insisted. "I want it examined by an expert."

A skilled locksmith was called in. But after a thorough inspection, he found nothing wrong with the time lock. Nor could he see any way of rendering it inoperative. But clinging to the only possibility that logic appeared to permit, Burns stubbornly refused to accept the local man's judgment. He wired Chief Wilkie that he wanted the Secret Service's own specialist sent out from Washington.

Then, proceeding on the assumption that the gold had somehow been stolen at night, he shut himself in his hotel room for an evening with the district office's preliminary file on the case, and the little floor-plan sketch and sparse observations he'd made in his notebook.

"Suppose I wanted to rob the mint?" he asked himself. "How would I go about it?" Point by point, he worked out a possible plan.

"I would have to be someone with a detailed knowledge of both mint operations and security precautions," he began. "I would also have to be a mint official so prominent and respected that I could enter the building after business hours, probably under the pretext of doing some overtime work, and arouse no suspicion.

"If I were such a person," he continued, "what would my plan be?

"I would have to know the combination of that vault legitimately, or else know where the combination was kept, and then manage to steal a look at it. I would also have to overcome the obstacle of the time lock. Then I would accustom the guards to the sight of my coming to work in the evenings. I would also begin carrying a container — something readily explainable and not unusual — in and out with me. I would do this until the guards grew careless and let me leave several times without an inspection.

"Then one night when I came out, the gold would be in that container.

"Would I have to leave and enter the cashier's department directly, in full sight of the watchmen at the main door and those patrolling the corridor as well?

"No," he decided after studying his sketch. "I could enter the chief clerk's department instead. Then, if I knew the exact timing of the various patrols, I could slip unseen into the superintendent's office and pick the right moment to duck across the 10-foot-wide hallway into the receiving room. I could climb over the counter there, go through the connecting door into the weighing room, then wait until a check of the cashier's department had just been completed. This would give me twenty minutes to open the vault, get the gold, and start back by the same roundabout way — still unseen if the timing were right."

This was a highly hypothetical plan making countless assumptions that couldn't be made as yet, raising more questions than it answered. But if was still a plan of sorts. So Burns next asked himself who might possibly have pulled it off.

Ignoring for the moment the obvious point that only one man was supposed to have known the vault combination, who at the mint would have both the knowledge and prominence that would be needed?

After studying the file from the district office for some time, Burns decided he really had only three possible suspects — Superintendent Leach himself, Chief Clerk Dimmick and Cashier Colton.

He began questioning this trio the next morning, and he began at the top. From the background material in the file, he knew that Frank Leach was one of the ablest and most highly regarded officials in the entire Treasury Department. The Superintendent had a long spotless record and enjoyed his work and his position. It was well-known that he had turned down numerous higher-salaried offers from private financial institutions.

"How often were the contents of the cashier's vault checked?" Burns asked him.

At the close of each working day, the superintendent explained. Normally, the cashier and the chief clerk made the count together. With Colton sick, he himself had helped Dimmick with the counting, and it was then that the shortage had been discovered.

Did that mean, Burns inquired, that the gold had been removed since the previous day's count?

Not necessarily, Leach admitted. The daily counts hadn't been accurate for some time. The vault had been unusually full for several months, and with all the wall compartments filled with sealed bags of coins, two hand trucks had been wheeled in against the back wall to provide more storage space. When Leach had made the count that day, he'd pulled back the truck and found two compartments empty behind them, with three bags of Double Eagles missing from each. Both Dimmick and later Colton had sheepishly admitted that they hadn't been moving the trucks on their counts for some time, that they'd simply been taking it for granted that all the hidden compartments were still filled.

"It was careless of them, of course," Leach added. "But it's just the sort of thing that happens when men work regularly with large amounts of money. They had been counting together every day for a year. And who would worry about bags of gold being stolen from a vault in the back corner of a United States Mint?"

"For a year, you say?"

91

Colton had become the cashier about a year ago, replacing Dimmick when Dimmick was promoted from cashier to chief clerk, Leach explained.

And the vault combination was changed at that time? Burns persisted. With the new combination known to no one but Colton, and the sealed envelope containing an emergency copy remaining unopened until the very day the shortage was discovered?

"That's true," the superintendent said defensively, "but Harold Colton couldn't possibly be suspected of something like this — or Walter Dimmick, either, for that matter. I regard both as fine young men. Dimmick is extremely able and has a brilliant future ahead of him. And I've never known a more conscientious employee than Colton."

Burns thanked the Superintendent, and walked over to chat with the chief clerk.

Still short of middle age, Walter Dimmick did indeed have a brilliant future ahead of him. He was personable, confident, and unabashedly ambitious. Previous investigation had disclosed that he lived at the very limit of his income in order to retain membership in several of San Francisco's most fashionable clubs, but this was hardly an unusual situation for a highly regarded official with every expectation of contined success. Dimmick's club memberships could, in fact, be regarded as a sound investment in his future. Perfectly at ease, he looked the Secret Service man straight in the eye as they talked.

Burns went over the same matters he had discussed with Superintendent Leach — the daily counts in the cashier's vault, the changing of the combination. Dimmick answered all questions readily and calmly. He mentioned that he had followed the news of the Pennsylvania counterfeiting conspiracy with interest and praised Burns' role in solving the case.

Bill Burns beamed. By the time he shook hands and left, they were talking like old friends.

92

Cashier Harold Colton was a different sort of man entirely — slim and intent, and by nature methodical. He appeared very nervous. The Secret Service had discovered nothing suspicious in his background, beyond the fact that his income also was stretched to the limit, but in his case chiefly because of family medical bills.

"I know it looks bad for me," Colton said. He twisted in his chair and lifted his eyes from his desk only occasionally. "But I didn't do it"

"If you didn't take the gold, who could have taken it?"

"I don't know," Colton said weakly. "No one else knew the combination."

"Suppose someone else had managed to learn that combination? Who would be familiar enough with the routine of your department to rob that vault? Dimmick, of course — since he so recently headed that same department. Superintendent Leach. Anyone else?"

Colton looked surprised. The thought of suspecting the superintendent was ridiculous, he argued. And why would a comer like Dimmick ever do such a thing? Colton could suggest nobody else, however.

Burns had met all the suspects. He also had worked out a method by which the crime might possibly have been committed. Now he had to begin testing it. He spent the next few days privately questioning each member of the 29-man security force. What officials and employees of the mint had recently been in the habit of returning to work in the evenings? The repeated answer was that a great many men had been doing this, Leach, Dimmick and Colton among them, for the mint had been unusually busy the past few months.

What about inspections? Had any package been carried out that seemed so routine it was passed through without being opened? Each of the guards shook his head stubbornly.

Burns appeared to have reached a dead end. His questioning continued, but the answers remained unchanged. With every employee feeling he might be under suspicion, the atmosphere grew strained and tense. Only the jovial Chief Clerk Dimmick went out of his way to be friendly and ask how the investigation was proceeding. Burns decided to throw the problem in his lap.

"You seem to be about the best-posted man in the place," he said. "Surely you must have some idea who might have taken the money."

Dimmick hesitated for a moment, and then conceded that Colton had to be the only person who conceivably could have committed the theft.

"But how could Colton or anyone else have done it?" Burns asked.

Dimmick confessed bewilderment, but he promised to ponder the question and try to arrive at some plausible answer.

Shortly afterward, the Secret Service's lock specialist arrived. Burns interrupted the monotonous and repetitious questioning to watch a gifted expert at work. The man completely disassembled the time lock at the cashier's vault and examined and tested its components. When he finished, one basic argument against Bill Burns' theory was erased.

"This time lock may be working now," the specialist reported, "but there was a period in the past when it wasn't." He went on to explain that a small nickel arm in the mechanism had been bent down so that it no longer engaged. It was later bent back into place, leaving traces of strain visible to anyone who knew the properties of nickel. The locksmith then examined the regular vault lock as well, but reported it in perfect working order, with no evidence that it had ever been otherwise.

Assured now that the vault could have opened at night with the right combination, Burns resumed his probe with fresh determination. On two occasions, Dimmick, true to his promise, took him aside to advance ideas of how the robbery could have occurred. It was possible, the chief clerk explained, that on a day when a number of large deposits were made in succession, the six bags of Double Eagles either were not registered or were intentionally ignored in the count. The thief might then have brought the extra bags out of the vault and hidden them somewhere — under a counter, perhaps — and covered them with empty sacks.

Burns discounted these theories on the grounds that the counting procedure he had witnessed was too foolproof, and also because there were too many employees everywhere to permit the bags to be taken out unnoticed during the daytime. Moreover, Dimmick still had no explanation as to how the coins could have been removed from the building.

Burns now was increasingly convinced that the money had been taken out of vault and building on the same night, and that the empty compartments hidden behind the wheel trucks in the vault explained why the theft could have been undetected for so long.

Back he went to his man-to-man questioning of the security force. Had anyone ever taken anything out of the mint that they hadn't taken in? Burns asked, over and over again. Had a container of any sort ever been allowed out without a thorough inspection?

As dull as his voice may have sounded the third or fourth time around, his senses were alert. A moment came at last when a guard seemed to hesitate a split second before answering in the familiar negative. And in doing so, the man shook his head a bit too emphatically, with fresh insistence in his denial instead of the toneless way others had been responding to the seemingly endless interrogation.

Burns bore in like a prizefighter spotting a cut above an opponent's eye. His voice became firm and threatening as he warned the guard that if he hid any evidence he faced the prospect of standing trial as an accomplice.

The guard finally broke down. He had just remembered that there was something he permitted to be carried out uninspected — not once but several times. But it couldn't have anything to do with the missing Double Eagle gold pieces. Some months earlier, an official of the mint had come in around 7 P.M., carrying a suitcase with a set of evening clothes in it. After doing some work, he used the mint building as a dressing room, changing in full sight of several guards, then left for some kind of social function. He returned about 11:00, used an office to change back into his business suit, then walked out carrying the formal clothing in his suitcase again. The social function evidently had been a regular affair, because the man had done the same thing a week later, and then during each of several weeks after that.

After five or six times, the guard admitted, he had begun waving the official by when he offered to open the suitcase upon leaving. The guard had known this was wrong and that he should have continued checking. But he'd felt foolish in going through the same routine time after time. He was just a guard, new on the force, in fact. And the man was the mint's chief clerk, Walter Dimmick.

In reviewing the case years later, Burns would say with a knowing smile that he always had a mild distrust of suspects who looked Secret Service operatives squarely in the eye, and a deep distrust of amateur detectives. The truth was that he *had* found the chief clerk a shade overfriendly; but as for the amateur detective work, Dimmick had only undertaken it at professional Burns' suggestion. It was dogged questioning and requestioning on the part of a great investigator that had revealed a key suspect. And now that Burns had his first solid clue, he pounced on it.

When was the last time that Dimmick had left with the suitcase? Burns asked the guard.

He couldn't be sure. Some time around St. Patrick's Day.

Warning the worried watchman not to repeat any of this until given permission to do so, the Secret Service man next interviewed the entire security staff again, gradually directing his questions to Dimmick and his activities. A few new pieces emerged to fit the puzzle. One watchman remembered that more than a year earlier, Dimmick had complained of some difficulty with the time lock on his vault and had worked on it himself an entire evening. Another recalled an evening in late March, just after St. Patrick's Day, when Dimmick had come out with his suitcase. The guard had offered to carry it down to the streetcar stop for him. The chief clerk refused the offer.

St. Patrick's Day was a long time back, but Burns had some luck when he began making inquiries among the conductors on the streetcar line. One of them had had several quarrels with "that crank from the mint," as he called Dimmick, and he'd made a note of their latest argument just in case a complaint was lodged against him. That argument had taken place when Dimmick boarded the car with an obviously heavy suitcase, then became angry when told it was blocking the aisle.

The car where this incident took place had been making a run to the ferry dock, and Burns' luck held out a little longer. A watchman there remembered offering to help a man of Dimmick's description with a heavy suitcase and being refused very emphatically.

The trail fizzled out on the far ferry dock. Dimmick had sent his family ahead on St. Patrick's Day vacation, Burns learned, but no one recalled his having a heavy suitcase when he finally joined them. The gold had apparently vanished en route.

Even then, Burns realized that he hardly had a case against the chief clerk. There was still the matter of the combination to the vault, known only to Harold Colton. Any defense attorney would be able to plant a reasonable doubt in a jury's mind on that point alone.

How had Dimmick learned the new combination? Was there any way, in turning the department over to Colton, that he could have fixed the lock?

Burns decided to have a talk with the locksmith who had set the dial on that occasion. The detective searched the files for the bill that had been presented to the mint. But there was no such bill.

"Colton," he told the cashier, "if you had a locksmith in to change the combination when you took over this department, he was a very generous fellow. He didn't charge the taxpayers a cent."

"But we didn't bring in a man," Colton said.

Burns looked at Colton in surprise. "The vault combination was changed, though. That's policy, and everyone, including you, insisted it was done."

"It was," the cashier explained indulgently. "I did it myself. Mr. Dimmick told me that there was no need to go to the expense because I could easily make the change just as he had done when he became cashier. He showed me how. There are only four numbers and the first and last are fixed. Only the two numbers in the middle had to be changed."

"Suppose you show me exactly what he showed you. Think hard and try to remember where both of you were standing at the time. Then I want to watch from where Mr. Dimmick was standing while you change the combination again."

By the time the demonstration was over, Burns had the case he needed. If Walter Dimmick hadn't been able to learn the new combination exactly, he'd at least been able to get a good enough idea of what the new middle numbers were to be able to open the vault after just a few tries.

There was nothing to be gained by delaying an arrest any longer. Dimmick had left the mint by then, but Burns found him later that evening in a small private room of a social club. Dimmick came out and greeted his visitor with a smile and a hearty handshake.

"Has something come up, Bill? Have you caught the gold thief?"

"Yes, Walter," Burns told him dryly. "You."

Dimmick laughed and kept insisting it had to be joke.

THE STAR OF THE SECRET SERVICE

Then he got angry. Finally, he began talking in a low, even voice.

"You see those fellows in there?" He nodded at the room he'd just left. "They're my friends, and they happen to be some of the most powerful men in this city. They can make or break people. Bigger men than you have lost their jobs by getting on the wrong side of them."

"I'll have to take that chance. Right now you're coming with me."

"I warn you, Burns," Dimmick snapped, forgetting they were on a first name basis. "Arrest me, and you'll be all through in the Secret Service."

For two days, Burns kept Dimmick a virtual prisoner in a hotel room, trying to talk him into signing a statement. But the man held out stubbornly.

"Suppose, just for the sake of discussion, I really did take that money," he did say once. "Would I go free, with all charges dropped if I returned it?"

This was more than Burns could promise, and there was no confession. When Dimmick went on trial, he was still vigorously protesting his innocence.

The case dragged on for nearly two years in the courts. The first jury failed to agree on a verdict. A new trial was ordered, and still another hung jury resulted. Washington was watching the case with more than normal interest. Burns was now back in the East, and one day his old friend Assistant Attorney General James Beck called him into his office.

"Is this man Dimmick really guilty?" Beck wanted to know.

"Of course he's guilty. He practically admitted it when he was fishing for a deal right after I arrested him."

"Then why can't we get a conviction?"

"Because the government is too cheap to assign enough men to keep a jury from being fixed," Burns said bluntly.

Beck went immediately to the Attorney General. The third jury was kept under close surveillance, and Walter

Dimmick ended up with five years in prison. But Burns' satisfaction in solving another "impossible" case was tempered by the fact that no trace was ever found of the suitcaseful of gold that had vanished from the San Francisco mint. He always felt that Dimmick buried the $30,000 in Double Eagles in some remote spot in the California countryside and never tried to recover it because he feared being apprehended again.

Interestingly enough, the social-climbing chief clerk's prediction about Burns being through in the Secret Service came true soon after the final trial — but hardly because of the political influence of San Francisco clubmen. On May 1, 1903, William J. Burns was transferred from the Treasury Department upon special request of President Theodore Roosevelt, to a newly created position in the Department of the Interior. There was strong reason to suspect that the nation was being systematically swindled out of vast holdings of public land in the West, and the President had borrowed the one investigator who, he was advised, would bring him the truth.

PART THREE

The Frauds in the Lieu-Lands

In wooded Tillamook County, Oregon, a Catholic priest named Joseph Schell listened to a plaintive tale. After long years of attempting to scrape their livelihoods from a stubborn land, of felling trees and pulling stumps and cutting brush, of fighting a wilderness that seemed to be trying to choke them out, a number of his homesteader parishioners had suddenly learned that the federal government would be taking back their marginal farms to make them part of a new forest preserve.

Father Schell nodded sympathetically. Such preserves were being established all over the West at the time. Conservation had become a matter of national concern; the United States finally was waking up to the fact that some if its wild beauty had to be safeguarded immediately or lost forever. But the northwoods priest knew that Congress had passed laws providing compensation for the dispossessed. Certificates were being issued, he explained, entitling those who lost land to choose and claim "in lieu thereof" an equal amount of public land elsewhere. Or the dispossessed could choose to be compensated in cash, if they wished, since these certificates, known as "lieu-lands scrip," were negotiable and of a high market value at the moment. Lumbering, mining and stock-raising interests were very eager to obtain them.

101

The troubled settlers hadn't finished their story, however. They had already learned about lieu-lands scrip, and they had gone to the state land office to fill out the proper papers. But they had been stunned to hear that their claims were not considered valid. Some legal difficulties existed that they didn't understand.

Joseph Schell was seriously concerned then. He was a priest, not a lawyer. But his parishioners had nowhere else to turn. Certain some minor error had occurred that could easily be cleared up, he made a trip to the state land office himself. And there he found himself as baffled as his parishioners had been. He was an educated man, but he couldn't understand the technical talk of title faults he heard from the officials he saw. While politely agreeing that a great injustice had been done, they insisted they were merely following the letter of the law, as they were required to do.

The priest refused to believe this. He began the difficult task of learning the law well enough to argue the point. Straining his eyes over borrowed books, he studied the involved passages until he not only understood but had committed to memory the lieu-lands laws and all other applicable pieces of legislation since the original homesteading act. Then, qualified to discuss the legalities with anyone, he returned to the land office.

Once again, he received no satisfaction. The officials declined to debate land laws with him. Instead, they took refuge in citing certain vague and complex administrative procedures they said they had followed, and firmly insisted the matter was closed.

Father Schell wasn't a suspicious man by nature, but he became suspicious then. He was even less a detective than a lawyer, but he turned detective with the same persistent patience. He discovered that strangers had recently filed claims to the homesteads where his people had lived for years, and that the land office had honored such claims. He learned that these strangers had immediately signed their rights over to a Portland banker who was prospering by speculating in lieu-lands scrip, and that a Portland attorney had prepared all the necessary papers beforehand. Blundering often but never giving up, the wilderness priest amassed facts and figures that strongly suggested a flagrant large-scale fraud had taken place, not within the letter of the law but far outside it. Confident that he would see justice done at last, he presented his findings to the proper Oregon authorities.

Nothing happened even then. He found himself being given the same answers he had received from the state land office officials, whom he now had reason to believe were being bribed by the Portland banker. Father Schell was not naive, but true to his vocation he did have a basic trust in the honesty of most men. It seemed incredible to him that the corruption could be so widespread. Yet soon after he revealed what he knew to the authorities, he began receiving anonymous notes threatening his life.

The threats didn't stop him. Nor was he stopped when the Portland lawyer who had engineered the swindle offered him a large amount of money, then brought out an affidavit in which a local woman falsely swore to misconduct on the priest's part. Father Schell could not be bribed or blackmailed. Even when his superiors in the Church suddenly transferred him without explanation, he went right on trying to right the wrong he claimed had been done the homesteaders who were no longer his parishioners. Since Oregon officials wouldn't help, he turned to a federal official — United States District Attorney John H. Hall. Hall brushed him aside with vague promises that were never kept. He went to the newspapers next. Editors took one glance at the names of some of the prominent men he said were guilty of fraud and shunted him aside as if he were a lunatic.

Father Schell then presented his case in a long, detailed letter to a high official whose honesty was beyond question — Secretary of the Interior Ethan Allen Hitchcock. The letter never reached Hitchcock's desk and was answered only with a formal acknowledgment from a minor clerk. Month after month went by and nothing happened. The Tillamook County settlers who had set their priest off on this lone crusade had long since been forced off their lands, without compensation.

Father Schell saw but one course left to him. He obtained a leave of absence and made the long trip across the country to Washington, D. C.

He tried to see Secretary Hitchcock first, but an Assistant secretary told him the charges he was making were a matter for the Justice Department, not Interior. When the priest obtained an interview with an assistant attorney general, he was sent back to the General Land Office in the Interior Department. There he tried to get an appointment with Commissioner Binger Hermann, whose assistants passed him on to Assistant Commissioner W. A. Richards, whose assistants sent him to the Lieu-Lands Division under William Valk. Valk's secretary referred him to the Forestry Division, headed by H. H. Jones, whose clerks decided the matter was properly the concern of Chief Harlan of the Land Office's special agents, who referred him on to other referrers — on and on in spiraling circles through the strange dreamlike labyrinth of a seemingly inexhaustible bureaucratic wasteland.

The knowing voices of underlings whose directions led nowhere rang in Father Schell's head when he tried to sleep at night. His days seemed nightmarish, with repetitious contradiction and confusion. He appealed to Senator John Mitchell of Oregon, then to his state's other U. S. Senator, Charles Fulton. Both had sympathetic secretaries, but neither senator ever seemed to be in when he called.

He wouldn't give up and go home. Somewhere in the maze of officialdom, he remained stubbornly certain, there was someone who would listen to the truth, then right a wrong done in the Oregon woods. The lower echelons of the Interior and Justice Departments made a game of bouncing him back and forth. After a time, Father Schell stopped listening to directions and simply began trying any office he couldn't remember entering earlier. He became the joke of Washington. He was "that crazy priest" in the lunch-hour laughter of innumerable petty clerks and secretaries, minor officials and other employees. Practically every receptionist in the nation's capital came to know him on sight. But even when he could no longer appear in public without being greeted by patronizing smiles or outright snickers, he kept right on trying.

By then, only one thing short of death could have stopped him — a direct order from his superiors. And such an order came. Church officials in Oregon called him back, transferred him a second time and soundly rebuked him for bringing ridicule upon himself and his garb. There was nothing more he could do.

Father Schell literally had been a voice crying in the wilderness, then a voice from the wilderness crying in Washington. And no one had listened. But with a patience and faith incomprehensible to most men, he accepted the judgment of his superiors as right and proper. He still believed that justice would be done, not in terms of his own vindication but for the defrauded homesteaders of Tillamook County. With a respectful eye to the proverbial mystery of the way the Lord works, he merely assumed that he wasn't the Lord's chosen instrument in this matter.

Father Schell was right. The mysterious instrument at the moment was a swindler, blackmailer and revenge-seeking informer named Joost R. Schneider, who was sitting at a table in Tucson, Arizona, and writing an angry letter to the General Land Office in Washington. Schneider had been the executive secretary to two millionaire California real estate promoters named John Benson and F. A. Hyde. He charged that the chief business of his former employers consisted of filing false claims to public land, then bribing federal forest superintendents to recommend new forest preserves that would include their claims, enabling them to obtain the valuable

105

lieu-lands scrip. He even asserted that the two wealthy partners had paid off some officials in Washington.

Schneider's accusations were hardly the first to reach the Land Office, and they were no more sensational and far less detailed than the charges Father Schell had so persistently presented. But the letter from Tucson arrived at an unusually opportune moment, at a time when ambitious Assistant Commissioner W. A. Richards was wondering how he could unseat and replace Commissioner Binger Hermann. Richards furtively made a copy of Schneider's letter before passing it on to his superior. He watched delightedly when Hermann merely filed the letter. He waited until enough time had passed to make it clear the Commissioner intended taking no action. Then he saw that the copy he had kept reached Secretary of the Interior Hitchcock.

A man whose Puritan righteousness occasionally made him a target for newspaper cartoonists, Hitchcock was furious. He called in Hermann and demanded to know why such scandalous allegations hadn't been reported to him immediately. Hermann had no satisfactory answer. Hitchcock indignantly demanded and received Hermann's resignation.

Richards' scheme had worked. He was the new Commissioner, and he dutifully ordered an investigation of Joost Schneider's letter — dispatching a Land Office agent to Tucson. But very abruptly, obviously because his former employers had agreed to meet his blackmail demands, Schneider had retracted all charges and stopped talking. Commissioner Richards reported this to Secretary Hitchcock, then relaxed triumphantly in his new office and did no more.

But Hitchcock had already told the story to President Theodore Roosevelt. Foreseeing the implications of the fraud, if indeed there was one, Roosevelt had ordered a special investigation and called in Secret Service Chief John Wilkie for consultation. Wilkie decided the situation called for a new force of outside investigators. To organize and command them, he offered to lend the Interior Department the much-

106

publicized solver of the recent counterfeiting and mint-robbery cases, his star operative William J. Burns.

Operating quietly and alone at first, with his identity known to no one in the General Land Office, Burns began by posing as a law school professor doing academic research on the mechanics of the lieu-lands statutes. For about two weeks, he did little more than familiarize himself with the details of the exact process by which claims for lieu-lands scrip came in from the field to Washington and were honored, as well as the methods by which recommendations for the establishment of forest preserves were made and accepted. Then he shocked the Secretary of the Interior and the President with his preliminary report.

"The General Land Office is corrupt at every level," he announced. "Corrupt to the very core"

What grounds did Burns have, Hitchcock demanded for a wholesale condemnation of the entire Land Office?

"When there's crookedness in a man's department, and he does nothing about it," Burns replied, "then he's either a crook himself or a fool. I've talked to most of the Land Office officials, and I don't think they're all fools."

"Well, we shall have to have more than theory, you know," the Secretary of the Interior said impatiently.

"You'll get more," Burns promised. "Those charges Schneider made were true. John Benson must be a silent partner, but the name of F. A. Hyde appears in the files on lieu-lands transactions so often that any honest man would have been suspicious. I don't see how that many claims could been approved without the help of William Valk in the Lieu-Lands Division and H. H. Jones in the Forestry Division. I don't see how the Land Office agents could have failed to investigate Hyde without Chief Harlan being in on the scheme as well. And what about Commissioner Richards, whose responsibility the whole business was?"

"Richards! Richards is the man who exposed Hermann

to me," Hitchcock reminded Burns. "Do you have any evidence at all?"

"No, and I'm not asking for indictments now," Burns told him. "I'm just telling you what to expect. The General Land Office is rotten from top to bottom."

Preparing to leave for Tucson, Burns requested an assistant. Since the Secret Service had separated him from his family during most of the last decade and a half, he had no hesitation in asking Chief Wilkie to have his son George detached from the New York District Office.

Tall, slim and strikingly handsome, 21-year-old George Edward Burns had proven a capable operative. He also had inherited his father's taste for the glamour that surrounded the stage. Already a familiar figure on Broadway, his social acquaintances were largely theatrical people, and one of his closest friends was playwright George M. Cohan. After three years in the Secret Service, however, he was itching for a chance to work with his celebrated father and the adventure he knew such an assignment would have to bring. His enthusiasm was only slightly subdued when the senior Burns warned him that what he would need most on this case would be a strong pair of legs.

George's main job in the weeks ahead, his father explained on the train, would be to pack some food, a camera and surveying instruments, load a tent and a sleeping bag on his back, then go hiking into the rugged mountains of the various forest preserves to examine the homestead claims for which lieu-lands scrip had been granted. If such claims were legal, the land would have to have been improved, meaning that dwellings had gone up and fields had been cultivated. If not, William J. Burns wanted photographic proof that the land had not been touched.

But first George got the chance to watch his father in action when they stopped at Tucson for a confrontation with Joost Schneider, whose letter had set off the probe. They

108

picked up the local postmaster to be a witness, but for a long time the interview with the sullen Schneider produced nothing worth witnessing. He kept repeating his second story, insisting his original accusations were false.

Then gradually, almost imperceptibly, the veteran detective began winning admission after admission from the man. The technique he was using consisted of making some outlandish charge, then arguing hotly when Schneider denied it. Finally, as if in defeat and resignation, the senior Burns would say, "Well, at least this much is true . . . ." and offer some minor obvious fact that Schneider had no reason to deny. Relieved at having the major accusation dropped, Schneider would generally agree. This became an established pattern. As George Burns listened in fascination, he heard the points to which Schneider was agreeing become steadily more significant. Before long, the man was admitting things he had angrily denied an hour or two earlier. By the time he realized what was happening and refused to say more or sign a statement, he had confessed, before the postmaster witness, practically all he had written in his letter.

Moving on to the coast, William J. Burns saw his son off on the solitary homestead-hunting trip, then hired some experienced California detectives, operatives he arranged to have detached from the Secret Service office at San Francisco. He also picked up men from various police departments and a few recommended private investigators. He put them to work shadowing and checking on promotors John Benson and F. A. Hyde, as well as a number of other suspects. These included their chief employees, customers for lieu-lands scrip, and several Land Office field men who fell in the "crooks-or-fools" category.

Some proved to be both. One forest superintendent had been blatantly padding his expense accounts. When Burns confronted him with this petty fraud, the man went on to admit the larger one he had committed by accepting bribes from Benson and Hyde. Other lines of attack brought similar confessions from another forest superintendent and a General Land Office special agent, plus evidence against a number of state officials which Burns turned over to the California attorney general. But perhaps most important, Bill Burns was getting an ever-clearer picture of the way this complex, large-scale swindling system worked.

The two wealthy real estate promotors, he discovered, had begun their operations by "settling dummies" upon public land: paying anywhere from $25 to $150 to individuals, usually derelicts from city saloons, to make false affidavits swearing that they had settled on wilderness claims and improved the land in accord with the homesteading laws. Benson and Hyde would then bribe Land Office officials, just as Schneider had said, to recommend forest preserves mapped out by the partners to include large numbers of these bogus claims. Once such recommendations had been accepted, with the "dummies" signing over the rights to their mythical homesteads in advance, the promotors would receive large quantities of lieu-lands scrip to sell to lumbering and mining interests, or more often to the railroads that were deeply involved in both businesses.

After a while, Benson and Hyde had gone further. With federal and state officials on their payroll, they had no hesitation about usurping the claims of legitimate homesteaders on occasion — as the Portland group had done to Father Schell's parishioners up in Oregon. Lately, Benson and Hyde had been saving themselves the cost of hiring tavern loafers by advertising for employees they had no intention of hiring, then forging the names and addresses of applicants on the various affidavits involved. In some cases, they had simply used fictitious names.

The full extent of the fraud became clearest when young George Burns came down from the mountains and rejoined his father. Lean and sunburned, he brought back photographic proof that every land claim in the Lake Tahoe Forest Preserve for which lieu-lands scrip had been issued was false, along with most of those in the Sierra, Zaca Lake and Pine Mountain preserves. He had photographs of alleged home-steads that were actually far above the permanent snow line. Included were pictures of a mountain few men had ever climbed, yet a dozen homesteads supposedly were located on top.

Bill Burns returned to Washington to face Secretary of the Interior Hitchcock and the President of the United States with another report. The President was red-faced with indignation as he read it. The very cause of conservation was being perverted, he stormed. Some of the most valuable lands in the West were falling into the hands of private exploiters, while such speculators in lieu-lands scrip as Benson and Hyde made fortunes by piously posing as champions of conservation who wished only to see the forests saved for posterity.

Who in Washington had been implicated in the several confessions of the field men? Roosevelt wanted to know.

Jones, Harlan and Valk, Burns told him.

"Not Hermann?" Hitchcock asked. "Why did he keep Joost Schneider's letter a secret then?"

"I don't know yet," Burns said. "Just how Hermann and Richards are connected to all this remains to be seen."

"Richards?" Secretary Hitchcock still protested the inference that the man who had exposed Hermann might be guilty himself.

"You go after everybody involved," the President cut in. "I'll back you up, no matter how highly placed they may be."

The first official Burns went after in Washington was H. H. Jones, head of the Forestry Division. Jones' protestations of innocence were both unconvincing and short-lived. Chief Harlan of the Land Office's special agents came next. The promptness with which he admitted accepting bribes from Benson and Hyde was astonishing. There are men, Burns had long ago learned, who almost seem to wait impatiently for a chance to confess. Harlan was just such a man.

111

William Valk, head of the Lieu-Lands Division, proved a different type of person entirely. Taking the initiative, Valk stalked into the office Burns was using and began raging that accusations were being cast his way and he wasn't going to stand for it. The detective was enough of an actor himself to recognize and respect a good performance when he saw one. He waited until Valk had blustered himself out, then motioned for a clerk to leave the room.

"Now I want to tell you something," Burns said. "I know the whole rotten situation here." He went on to describe the massive frauds he had uncovered, returning to the essential question of how false lieu-lands claims could be processed on such a scale without the head of the Lieu-Lands Division being either corrupt or feeble-minded. Confronted by these facts, Valk's protests grew weaker. In the end, white-faced and trembling, the man who had come to stage a show of outraged innocence confessed that he too had been paid off by the two West Coast promoters.

This confession had come just in time. One of Burns' California operatives wired that John Benson was on his way to Washington, apparently to learn the scope of the threat the new investigation posed for him. From the moment Benson stepped off the train, his every movement was watched. As expected, Benson dispatched a messenger to William Valk. Burns entered Valk's office soon afterward.

"Benson wants to see me," the Lieu-Land's Chief said. "What should I do?"

"Go see him."

"What if he offers me more money?"

"Take it and bring it to me." Burns gave other instructions, making it clear that he wanted Valk to put on as convincing an acting performance as he had demonstrated when he stormed into Burns' office.

Valk did as he was told, visiting Benson alone in a hotel room and assuring him that the special investigation had produced nothing that could hurt the Californian — predicting, in fact, that the probe soon would be called off entirely.

Benson was relieved and grateful. During the meeting, he excused himself to use the bathroom. He came back grinning. "Don't you have to go in there too?" he suggested.

William Valk took the hint and found a $100 bill on the wash basin, which he later turned over to Burns to be marked and kept as evidence. A similar meeting with Chief Harlan produced a $200 bribe. More than enough of a case had been accumulated for the arrest of John Benson, and the indictment of his partner F. A. Hyde and two of their associates.

The Attorney General's office decided to grant immunity from prosecution to the several corrupted officials in return for their testimony as government witnesses. The case was assigned to a special prosecutor named Francis J. Heney, who had a reputation for both vigor and incorruptibility. Burns was sent back to the West Coast to assist Heney with extradition proceedings against Hyde and the others, but the President and the Secretary of the Interior felt that his investigation was largely completed. They already were congratulating him on a job well done.

But Burns had a strong feeling that the congratulations were premature. For one thing, he had failed to connect former Commissioner Binger Hermann to the land frauds, and he wasn't willing to shrug off as incompetence Hermann's suppression of an informer's letter as Secretary Hitchcock now was doing. For another, he had failed to implicate Commissioner W. A. Richards, as he had promised to do; and he still disagreed with Hitchcock's repeated contention that Richards' exposure of Hermann was evidence of innocence. He refused to believe that either Hermann or Richards could have been blind to all that was going on, and he was positive that there had been far more to it than was uncovered. A majority of homestead claims in California forest preserves had proven false. Almost certainly, the same system had spread to other areas of the West.

Burns discussed his suspicions regularly on the Coast with special prosecutor Heney, whom he discovered to be a fascinating partner. A bespectacled prim-appearing man, Frank Heney looked like a school teacher, and indeed he had been one on occasion. But in this case, looks were deceiving. Raised in a tough lowerclass neighborhood — "South of the Slot" in San Francisco — Heney had roamed the West as a jack-of-many-trades. He had been a cowboy, a prospector and an Apache trader, and he had once killed a man in a fight in Tucson. When he had finally settled down long enough to study and practice law, he had entered reform politics and gone on to the Attorney General's office. As Heney and Burns worked together through most of a court term, the prosecutor listened carefully to Burns' suspicions.

One day he mentioned that a land-fraud case soon would be coming to trial in Oregon. The case was small time in comparison to the Benson-Hyde affair. The accused were a gang of five petty claim jumpers headed by a woodsman named Steve Puter. U.S. District Attorney John Hall had dug up the evidence and secured the indictments, and he seemed to have things well in hand.

Burns wasn't so sure. Even millionaire operators like Benson and Hyde, he argued, were in effect only agents of interests eager to obtain lieu-lands scrip. He doubted, in light of all he'd seen in California, that land-fraud schemes to the north necessarily were minor affairs. He said that it would probably take another full-scale investigation to learn the whole truth.

When the extradition business in California was completed, Burns decided to follow his hunch. He obtained permission from Secretary of the Interior Hitchcock for another probe similar to the one he'd organized in California and asked Heney to join him. Retaining many of the same detectives he had used before, Burns established headquarters in Portland and once again sent his son George on a wilderness camping trip with a camera. Burns and Heney soon learned that the Puter group was simply the small portion of the iceberg above the surface; not only railroads and real estate

114

men but also a good many politicians were dealing in lieu-lands scrip. George W. Brownell, president of the state senate and the political boss of Oregon, for example, was very much involved in public lands manipulations. And almost immediately, Burns' crooks-or-fools theory made him increasingly suspicious of District Attorney John Hall.

"Hall couldn't possibly have believed there was no more going on here than the Puter gang's operation," he argued.

Heney didn't agree. "I know Hall isn't being very cooperative, but he's jealous of his prerogatives. He uncovered the Puter case, and he resents us. That's why I'm staying behind the scenes and letting him handle it."

But Burns' suspicions only hardened as the investigation went on. One day, as Burns was questioning an elderly forest superintendent named Ormsby, the district attorney suddenly opened the door of the office Burns was using, apologized for interrupting, then asked if he could speak to Ormsby outside for a moment. That moment was a decisive one. Until the interruption, the forest superintendent had been a cooperative witness and seemed to be on the verge of making an important admission. When he returned, whatever he had intended saying went unsaid.

"But why would Hall want to interfere with the gathering of evidence that could help him win his own case?" Heney asked, when he heard of the incident.

"Because he's a crook. I don't think he wants the Puter gang convicted."

"Then why did he have them arrested and indicted in the first place?"

"I don't know yet," Burns answered, "but I think you better take over the case yourself. And I have a hunch that if ever you've fought for a conviction, you'd better do it this time."

When the Puter trial began, Heney, in his role as special prosecutor, began questioning and cross-examining all witnesses, overriding the angry protests of District Attorney John Hall. Meanwhile, special detective Burns went after Superintendent Ormsby again. He blended threats of prison and promises of immunity with the skill of long experience. The official finally broke down and confessed what he had almost admitted in their earlier session — that he had let an agent of the Northern Pacific Railroad map out the Blue Mountain Forest Preserve for him. But it wasn't really his fault, Ormsby said. He had been ordered to do this by former Commissioner Binger Hermann, who had been west on a vacation at the time.

Hermann had finally been implicated, and this brought no gasp of surprise from Burns. Nor did it shock him to learn that a newly-elected congressman named Williamson, who controlled a number of claims just outside the preserve, as almost his first action in the House introduced a bill to have the Blue Mountain boundaries extended for his own benefit. With state boss Brownell setting the pace, politics and lieu-lands speculation seemed to be synonymous in Oregon.

But several essential questions were still unanswered. What did all this have to do with the petty Puter case? What was District Attorney Hall's part in the affair? Why had Hall attempted to suppress the information? Most puzzling of all, why had he arrested a bunch of small-time land thieves he didn't intend convicting?

As a threat? Or a form of blackmail? Certainly Puter and his confederates weren't worth threatening or blackmailing. Could it be that Hall was using his prosecution of the Puter gang as a weapon against someone the defendants could conceivably implicate if convicted? Someone from whom Hall himself wanted a favor?

This last thought stuck in Burns' mind because of a rumor included in several investigative reports on state boss George Brownell. In return for Brownell's help with their campaigns, it seemed, Oregon's two United States Senators,

John Mitchell and Charles Fulton, had jointly promised their benefactor the first available appointment as U.S. District Attorney — an obviously valuable asset for a lieu-lands speculator. Yet for some mysterious reason, that promise had never been kept.

Why not? Burns wondered. A quick query to Washington brought the interesting information that the only federal District Attorney in Oregon with a term nearing expiration at the time was John Hall. Had Hall been using the Puter gang prosecution as a threat by which he held on to his job? Did this mean that Steve Puter or his friends knew something that could implicate the powerful Brownell? Or Mitchell? Or Fulton? Or all three?

By now, Burns had the means to find out. His small army of detectives had gained the confidence of several disgruntled clerks and underpaid secretaries in Oregon's highest offices. One day a detective handed Burns a very revealing letter, obtained from a source Burns understandably never disclosed. The letter was addressed to George Brownell and read:

> I can assure you we are both anxious to discharge in some proper way the great obligations we are both under to you. I have received your several dispatches since Hall left Portland, and both Senator Fulton and myself have done everything in our power to protect you . . . . Of course, friend Brownell, this letter to you is in the strictest confidence. The best way for the present is to drop all talk about the District Attorney-ship; let the matter stand for the present. Both Fulton and I have, for the purpose of protecting your interest gone very much further in a certain direction than we ever thought we would. I cannot explain fully to you until I see you just what I mean. Hall leaves this evening for home. My advice would be for you to say nothing to him unless he says something to you. Just let the

matter drift for the moment. This is all-important.

John H. Mitchell

I have read the above and fully concur in it.
C.W. Fulton

There was actually nothing in this note that could be used in court, but it told Burns what he wanted to know: that claim jumper Steve Puter or one of his allies knew something which John Hall could use to retain his District Attorney's post. It now was more vital than ever to obtain a conviction in the Puter case. With the help of one of the several sets of photographs that young George Burns brought down from the mountains, Frank Heney won a verdict of guilty.

While Puter awaited sentence, Bill Burns went to work on him. The prisoner was a tight-lipped man whose personal code permitted dispossessing homesteaders but revolted at the notion of turning state's evidence. Still, Puter was an outdoorsman; he had threatened to kill himself before submitting to prison. His dread of being caged gave Burns the needed opening.

"Puter will get the limit," prosecutor Heney helpfully predicted to the newspapers, "in the penitentiary."

The convicted man's brother, Clarance Puter, was desperately attempting to raise bail by making the rounds of men for whom Steve had obtained fraudulent land claims. But at the same time, Burns' detectives were spreading a rumor that a new series of arrests was imminent, particularly if certain suspects could be connected with the prisoner. The Burns man shadowing Clarence reported that the bail seeker was having no luck getting money. Bill Burns waited a while longer, then called on Clarence.

"The big fellows are making a fall guy out of your brother," Burns snorted. "They want him in jail, out of the way. Now Heney's on to the whole layout, and he

118

doesn't want Steve and that bunch. He wants the big guns, the fellows who've gone back on Steve. And if you don't believe they've quit him, go and see. Try any of them."

"I have tried them," Clarence Puter had to concede bitterly. "I've tried them all."

Taking Clarence along, Burns had a long session in the jailed man's cell. He painted a grim word picture of years to be spent in prison. Against this, he promised that Puter would only have to pay a fine if he cooperated with the prosecution.

A man couldn't inform on his friends, Steve Puter kept protesting.

"Of course," Burns would soothingly agree. "But only if they really are friends, friends who'll stand by him."

Steve Puter was convinced. And once he started talking, he seemed unable to stop. He gave the names of dozens of people he had paid to sign false affidavits. He produced a little notebook in which he had listed the bribes given various officials. He even admitted using a lady friend in his work, pimping her off to government men whose help he needed.

As Burns had expected, Puter had a great deal of useful information about state boss George Brownell's public lands dealings. And Puter also knew something about Oregon's senior U.S. Senator, John H. Mitchell. He said that Mitchell, in return for two $1,000 bills, had once directed him to a high General Land Office official who supervised, for an additional price, the processing of some fraudulent land claims. That official, Burns heard with the feeling of a man nearing the end of a long trail, was the official that Secretary Hitchcock had refused to believe was corrupt, the man who had exposed and replaced his superior — Commissioner W. A. Richards.

All of the puzzle pieces fitted now, and Burns had the outline of his full case at last. The charges he had originally made about the Land Office had been understatement, not exaggeration; the same corruption had spread into both houses of Congress. He set his men determinedly to work document-ing and expanding that outline. New evidence and further confessions poured into his Portland office on a production-line basis, and he summarized and organized the material for prosecutor Frank Heney to use in obtaining indictment after indictment from a federal grand jury.

A routine case against five minor land thieves had ex-ploded into criminal charges against some of the most promin-ent men in Oregon. Powerful forces made frantic attempts to undermine Burns and Heney in Washington. But Secretary Hitchcock and President Roosevelt stood stubbornly behind them. The newspapers of the Northwest caricatured the federal detective-prosecutor team viciously, day after day. Then the situation grew still uglier. Word came to Burns that two professional killers from San Francisco had turned up in Portland. Frank Heney was their target, since the interests or men who hired them evidently reasoned that the investi-gation was largely accomplished while the prosecution was still to come. Despite Heney's protests, Burns assigned him bodyguards, and made a point of keeping a protective eye on the prosecutor himself. This perpetual armed guard finally frightened the gunmen off, but an attempt was made to des-troy Heney in a subtler way. Burns learned that a local lady had been hired to try to compromise Heney by swearing she had spent a night in a roadhouse with him. By publiciz-ing the plot in advance, Heney's moral reputation remained pristine, a serious matter in a day when scandal of this sort could have discredited him in the public eye and perhaps forced him to withdraw from the case.

Frank Heney believed that all of the lands-fraud prosecu-tions would succeed or fail with the oucome of the indictment against the most distinguished defendant, Senator John H. Mitchell. Sitting regularly beside Heney at a courtroom counsel table, Burns soon found that his own work was by no means finished when the senator's trial got underway. The prosecu-tion had produced checks, for example, that were payments for Mitchell's help in various lieu-lands manipulations. The checks were drawn to the law firm of Mitchell & Tanner. In a surprise move, the defense countered with a typewritten contract, dated the year of the senator's election, which stated that all the partnership's profits were to go solely to Tanner while Mitchell held public office. It was clear that any chance of a conviction was lost unless the contract was discredited.

Burns immediately put men to work tracing the manufacture of the paper on which was written the contract which legally exonerated Senator Mitchell from the activities of his own law firm. Burns hoped that his men would discover that the paper was produced after the date on the contract. It was a long shot, and Burns realistically recognized that even if this were the case the trial probably would be over before he could get the necessary evidence.

In the meantime, he noticed that three different words were repeatedly misspelled on the contract. He also learned that the law firm had recently replaced a veteran stenographer with Tanner's own son. Questioned by Heney on the stand, the young man firmly denied that he had written and misdated the contract. But when asked in court to write out a sample sentence Burns had rigged up, he made the same spelling errors. By the time proof arrived that the contract had indeed been written on paper manufactured long after Mitchell took office, such proof was superfluous. To save his son from a threatened perjury indictment, Tanner had already confessed that the agreement was written after Mitchell's indictment.

Months of work had been salvaged by a shady law firm's carelessness and a great detective's eye for error. Senator John Mitchell was convicted. He posted bond, appealed the conviction, and died while the appeal was in progress. Burns was back in Washington, making another report to the President, when word of Mitchell's death arrived. One story has it that Theodore Roosevelt was deeply depressed by the news.

"A crooked United States Senator is still a United States Senator," the President is reported to have said with considerable remorse.

"A crooked United States Senator, Mr. President," Burns is supposed to have answered, "is a crook."

The anecdote may well be apocryphal; it has too neat a ring to be accepted unquestioned. But whether or not Burns' righteousness was as ruthless as the story would suggest, he and Francis J. Heney saw no reason to mourn Mitchell with any moratorium on the Oregon prosecutions. For more than two years, they labored together to secure a total of more than one hundred indictments. And of the thirty-four cases that went to trial while they worked as a team, thirty-three ended with convictions.

The two men left Portland together in the late summer of 1906. A new assignment awaited them in city streets instead of the nation's forest preserves. But even while moving on without pause to another large-scale investigation, Burns could grin at one final irony of the lieu-lands case.

He had long since heard the story of "that crazy priest" from Tillamook County, who had sought justice for some impoverished homesteaders, only to be buffeted from bureaucrat to bureaucrat, mocked and ridiculed by half the clerks and secretaries in Washington, then transferred and rebuked by his own superiors. Now, Burns heard the Oregon authorities of his Church proudly proclaim that "it was a priest, the Reverend Joseph Schell, who first called attention to the land frauds."

PART FOUR

Four Willful, Obstinate Men

On December 1, 1905, a rangy, rawboned man who looked like a frontier marshall but was actually a crusading newspaper editor called on President Theodore Roosevelt at the White House. His name was Fremont Older, his newspaper was the San Francisco *Bulletin,* and his mission was an ambitious one: he had come to ask federal help in cleaning up as graft-ridden a government as any American city has ever endured.

Roosevelt knew something of the situation. He'd heard most of the current San Francisco jokes; how, on the night of the last election, every burglar alarm in the city had gone off of its own accord; how the Board of Supervisors had once refused to listen to the Lord's Prayer because the customary bribes hadn't been paid; how the violin-playing mayor not only fiddled while the city burned, but was stealing and selling the fire-hoses as well. San Francisco had become nationally known as a place where corruption had been carried to the point of comedy and beyond.

Turning serious and sympathetic, the President asked what he could do to help. The editor couldn't be accused of thinking small. What he wanted was the President's personal, headline-producing detective, the star operative Roosevelt had borrowed from the Secret Service and turned loose in the

Interior Department with such momentous results. Older wanted special investigator William J. Burns sent to San Francisco, along with his skilled team of assistants and special prosecutor Francis Heney.

The President frowned thoughtfully. The crusading editor's idea had its attraction, and not just for the sheer spectacle of battle it promised. Roosevelt himself had been happily crusading on a national scale — loudly and usually effectively — busting trusts, denouncing "malefactors of great wealth," and swinging his now-famous Big Stick at government and corporate corruption alike. He had long hoped to inspire similar campaigns in the large cities of the nation.

Even so, he had to point out that he couldn't legally assign federal agents to clean up one city. As crooked and plunderous a pack as San Francisco's politicians might be, they were probably violating no federal law.

"Suppose private funds could be found to finance an investigation?" Older persisted. "Would you release Mr. Burns and Heney to undertake it?"

Roosevelt could only remind his visitor of the old recipe for rabbit stew: the first step was to get the rabbit. This was all the encouragement the newspaperman needed. Both Burns and Heney were in Washington at the time, and he called on them at the Willard Hotel the next day. He was already acquainted with Heney, a fellow San Franciscan. The special prosecutor was enthusiastic about Fremont Older's idea and introduced him to Burns.

Like most newsmen who met the country's front-page detective for the first time, Older was surprised by what he saw. The *Bulletin* had carried detailed accounts of Burns' major cases but the press photos made him seem a much larger man, dark-haired and ponderous. In person, the celebrated sleuth was, of course, short; and while stocky, he still was trim and athletic rather than portly. His hair and mustache remained a fiery red. He looked at least a decade younger than his 47 years. He had abrupt gestures, an electrifying briskness and compelling geniality.

"A large-scale investigation financed by public-spirited citizens?" Burns smiled but shook his head at the novel idea. During his two and a half years on special assignment for the President, he had built up a unique force of capable investigators, most of them family men. And having spent fourteen previous years in the Secret Service, working his way slowly up to a top salary of $7 a day while raising five children, he understood their problems. "I'll not be asking my men to depend on donations for their wages," he said firmly.

Fremont Older was a man chasing a dream. He returned to San Francisco determined to find a way to guarantee that the investigation he proposed would be adequately financed. He brought back the answer some months later — in the person of a young bank president named Rudolph Spreckels, a handsome if stiff-mannered aristocrat who had broken with a wealthy father and amassed his own fortune, chiefly in Hawaiian pineapple. Spreckels was just 36, but he had been a self-made millionaire for fully a decade, and he was fervently interested in Older's project. If other civic-minded citizens failed to join in footing the bill, Spreckels promised he would go it alone. Would it cost $100,000? $200,000? He stood to deposit the money in advance.

Burns still wasn't fully convinced. To break an organized graft system of any size, he explained to Spreckels, it was invariably necessary to grant immunity to bribe-taking petty officials in return for their testimony against the bribe payers. "Will you still be with us if we go after the big guns in San Francisco?" he wondered. "The corporations that corrupted the city? We could well be indicting and prosecuting some of your friends and fellow club members."

The millionaire's enthusiasm was undimmed. He would even go farther, he said. He hoped that the proposed investigation would eventually reach beyond the tainted city's borders and break up the railroad-dominated clique that had controlled California's politics for decades. With three eager men urging Burns on, the detective finally agreed to leave government service temporarily and lead the investigation.

Although he and Heney would be busy in Oregon for another court term, he promised to send a squad of his operatives to San Francisco immediately.

The meeting ended without a written agreement of any sort. There were merely handshakes all around by a crusading editor, an idealistic financier, a dedicated prosecutor and a deceptively genial detective. "Four willful, obstinate men," the nationally-famed journalist Lincoln Steffens would soon be calling them, first in admiration, then in astonishment, finally in exasperation. Those handshakes were to prove incredibly enduring.

Neither the tremendous earthquake that shook San Francisco on April 18, 1906, nor the great fire that raged for days afterward was allowed to interfere with the city officials' unique but established way of doing business. For example, a national trolley trust known as United Railroads had long been seeking a profitable local franchise. Urging municipally-owned transportation instead, a group of prominent citizens, Rudolph Spreckels among them, had offered to set up trolley lines and sell them to the city at cost. With public attention diverted by a natural disaster, the city fathers provided a man-made one. United Railroads got its franchise — for a secret price of $200,000. Of this, $85,000 was divided among 18 members of the Board of Supervisors, and $50,000 went to the violin-playing mayor, a handsome black-bearded rogue named Eugene Schmitz. But significantly enough, the largest share of the bribe, fully $65,000, went to a man who held no official position himself — a comic-looking, bushy-mustached little lawyer named Abraham Ruef.

Ruef was an apostate Republican who had failed in an attempt to seize power in his own party and had then taken over an obscure and faltering organization known as the Union-Labor Party, stunning everyone with his incredible success. He had little liking for the men he had put into office, but he had used them to make himself the absolute political

126

ruler of San Francisco. He was so secure in that role by the time the streetcar franchise was granted that he openly accepted, on a daylit public street, a graft payment so large that a special order had gone in to the local U.S. Mint which also served as a sub-treasury, to amass it.

Ruef had requested small bills and the heavy bundles of currency were turned over to him by a United Railroads attorney named Tirey L. Ford on May 25. Ruef calmly put the $65,000 in his new green limousine and drove away.

But already, a Burns detective was watching and listening. And another would soon be driving that eye-catching automobile as Ruef's personal chauffeur. Ten days earlier, offices had been quietly leased in the Gladstone Apartments at Polk and Eddy Streets by George Burns, just turning 24 but already a veteran of three years in the Secret Service and nearly three more as his father's chief assistant. And George was soon joined by another Burns boy. Twenty-year-old Raymond had grown bored with studying law at Ohio State and wanted to be in action. All through that summer, William J. Burns' two oldest sons worked with a growing group of his investigators, shadowing the various officials and cultivating the confidence of key clerks and secretaries.

When Burns and Heney came south from Portland, a detailed "graft map" of San Francisco was waiting for them. Burns then brought the investigation out into the open with a public announcement, prominently printed and regularly repeated by Fremont Older in the *Bulletin:* an offer of full immunity from prosecution to any citizen who felt he had been forced to pay graft to a city official and was willing to testify about it.

Predictably enough, the only response came from graft-paying citizens whose businesses were illegal anyway.

San Francisco was then noted for some exotic houses of ill repute known as "French restaurants," where gourmet food actually was served — on the first floor only. As generous as the French restaurant owners had always been with the local police, it seemed that they had suddenly found their liquor licenses revoked the year before. Upon protesting to Mayor Schmitz, they had been solemnly advised to consult an attorney who specialized in "municipal affairs" — attorney Abraham Ruef. Only after retaining Ruef for a fee of $5,000 a year had they been able to get their licenses restored.

Bill Burns listened to these gentlemen as sympathetically as if they were church deacons. He realized that their first-hand accounts provided an exact outline of the way San Francisco's graft system worked. There were a variety of private arrangements, but the big payments made by utilities and other concerns seeking franchises — as the preliminary reports of his men had made clear — also were invariably "legal fees" for boss Ruef's advice on municipal affairs, furtively shared with his puppet officeholders later.

"Ruef is the key to everything," Burns told Heney, Older and Spreckels. "He is the only link between the buyers and sellers. There's no need to do anything more to members of the Board of Supervisors than expose them and force them out of office. Most of them were laborers and workingmen before the last election, and they're having more money waved under their noses at every board meeting now than they used to make in a year. Instead of sending them to prison, we should use them to get Ruef. But the thing is, we can't use them to get the men who've been waving the money. The only way to the higher-ups is through Ruef himself." He paused a moment to let the problem sink in. "In the end, we'll have to make Abe Ruef *our witness*"

This was long-range strategy. The most immediate problem was to obtain some form of official status for Frank Heney, enabling him to get a special grand jury convened. Fortunately, the local district attorney held one of the few offices beyond Union-Labor Party control. The occupant owed his only political allegiance to publisher William Randolph Hearst and had been allowed to run without Ruef opposition in the last election as part of a deal whereby Hearst's San

Francisco *Examiner* had endorsed Mayor Schmitz in return. Once Heney made a trip eastward and convinced Hearst that backing the investigation would put him on both the winning and newsworthy side, an appointment as deputy district attorney was a mere formality.

Burns expected Ruef to fight Heney's appointment with every weapon at his command, including the police and sheriff's departments, but no one was prepared for the move that Ruef suddenly made. On October 25, he had his Board of Supervisors dismiss the district attorney and name Ruef himself as the replacement.

Ruef had stepped too far. By so blatantly grabbing the office, he had accomplished more for the graft investigation overnight than its four key figures could have done in months. The clean government forces now raced into action. Fremont Older published a blazing *Bulletin* extra that brought angry mobs into the streets, and Rudolph Spreckels found furious citizens joining his cause in increasing numbers. Burns seized the district attorney's office, barricading the doors and windows and posting his armed operatives to defend the building like a fort against Ruef's policemen and deputies. And Frank Heney had little difficulty getting a court injunction prohibiting any attempt by Ruef to act as district attorney.

With popular support rallied behind them, Heney impaneled a grand jury and Burns brought in his only waiting witnesses, the French restaurant owners. The witnesses may have been of questionable character but their testimony about payoffs wasn't. On November 15, both Abraham Ruef and Mayor Eugene Schmitz were indicted on five counts of extortion each. (The mayor was off on a lavish European vacation at the time, with young George Burns a grateful beneficiary because he'd been assigned to follow him every trans-Atlantic mile; Schmitz denounced the charges and started home immediately.) The first campaign in the war on San Francisco's corruption appeared to be a striking triumph for the investigators.

But Bill Burns was deeply worried. He didn't enjoy pitting himself against a man he didn't understand, and Ruef seemed to defy understanding at the moment. Why, Burns wondered, did this previously all-powerful little man seem delighted with what he'd done? Free on bond, he cruised smilingly about the city in that long green automobile as if he had no worries. Yet the detective knew that Ruef's craftiness bordered on genius; he had proven this conclusively with the intrigues and manipulations that had brought him control of San Francisco's government. Why then had he forsaken his backstage role and thrown himself into the public spotlight — generally shunned by grafting bosses — in such a startling and seemingly self-defeating manner?

Burns didn't know, and he didn't like not knowing. As he'd told his associates, Ruef was the key to everything. Unless he could be made to talk, the investigation was doomed to scratch only the surface. And Burns knew that he was still a long way from controlling this mysterious key.

One December day, while watching a crowd of Union-Labor Party regulars stream out from a political meeting, Burns noticed a tall, dark-haired local businessman who seemed to be on a first name basis with practically every officeholder in the current city government. Through history, there have been many people who ostensibly had a photographic memory. In Burns' case, it was the truth. He recognized the man immediately. His name was now Golden M. Roy. A decade earlier, when he'd ducked out on a still-pending forgery charge in Oklahoma, it had been Roy Moritz Golden.

Burns did not hesitate to use this information. While he had been riding with white knights of reform lately, he was still essentially a professional detective. And a detective's tactics often meant beating crooks at their own game. If the task of cleaning up San Francisco called for some blackmail, a blackmailer he would be. Working with Fremont Older a few nights later, he set up a *Bulletin* front page story with a headline that read: PROMINENT BUSINESSMAN EXPOSED AS

130

FUGITIVE FELON. But the type was uncased after printing a single copy, and that copy was shown only to Golden Roy.

The man was shocked, then furious. "That was ten years ago" he protested. And he bitterly reminded Burns that he had since become a respected family man, prospering in legitimate business.

Burns didn't bother reminding the fugitive forger, in turn, that he had prospered chiefly by supporting a corrupt municipal government. They both already knew it. The detective only said, with a genial grin, that he was certain such a respected family man would want to do his civic duty and not be as derelict as he himself had been by failing to wire the Oklahoma authorities immediately.

"What do you want me to do?" Roy asked in dull resignation.

Actually, Burns had no assignment ready. But he assured his new undercover man that something would turn up. Emphatically and dramatically, something did.

Burns had long ago learned that a detective had to pick up his tools where found them, and a really good detective could find some unlikely tools. One morning he noticed in his newspaper that a local priest had launched a campaign against roller-skating rinks, calling them sinks of degradation where innocent girls met lecherous men with predictable results.

Banning roller skating in San Francisco of that era was like outlawing wine in Gomorrah. But Burns was a staunch Catholic and only too happy to help. With Frank Heney's assistance, he drew up draft legislation to bar minor females from skating rinks unless chaperoned, a restriction that would have bankrupted every rink in the city. Then he saw that this ordinance reached the Board of Supervisors, with no hint of its source.

He was certain the city fathers would seriously consider the bill, since it would give them a chance to proclaim themselves publicly on the side of innocence and virginity after the late-October debacle in which Ruef had involved them. At the same time, Burns also believed that greed would prevail. He guessed that this was exactly the sort of petty matter in which the supervisors might be tempted with a lion's share commission. Most important, among the several legitimate enterprises of Golden Roy was a partnership in San Francisco's largest roller-skating establishment, the Dreamland Rink.

Burns quickly set the stage. Having obtained a leading man by means that bordered on blackmail, he rehearsed him for a performance a criminal lawyer could have called entrapment — if there had been any intention of prosecuting the men he intended trapping.

"I want you to offer the supervisors $500 apiece to vote against that bill," Burns said. He instructed Roy to try Supervisor Thomas Lonergan first.

Tom Lonergan was a former delivery-wagon driver who had once angered Abe Ruef by openly boasting he would retire with at least $100,000 in the bank at the end of his two-year, $100-a-month term. Lonergan readily agreed to drop in at Roy's office in the Dreamland one early February evening. Burns had arrived earlier. Drilling three peepholes through a side door of that office, he planted himself and a pair of stenographers out of sight behind it. When Lonergan came in, Burns was ready to preserve every word of the conversation.

"Tom" Roy began, "we skating-rink men have made up a purse to pay you people for beating this ordinance." He spoke loudly and slowly as ordered. "Will you stand in?"

"Sure." Lonergan pushed back his chair and lounged lazily in it.

Roy reached over and pulled him back into sight of the viewing slit. "Here's your money. Five hundred dollars. Is that right?"

"That's right", Lonergan said. He appeared a bit puzzled by the close-range shouting, but he wasn't suspicious. "I'll be your friend for as long as you live, Roy."

"There is no writing, of course," Golden Roy added as instructed, "so it must be understood between us that you accept this money and you agree in consideration thereof to vote against that ordinance."

The supervisor seemed mildly surprised by this belaboring of the obvious, but he agreed readily enough. Before leaving, he even tried to save some of the other supervisors the trouble of coming down by collecting their money for them.

Roy refused, insisting that he wanted a personal understanding with each man.

Once Supervisors Ed Walsh and Charles Boxton had accepted the same bribe as Lonergan, Burns had all the evidence he needed. One by one, he confronted the supervisors with the stenographers' transcripts. Surprised and frightened, all three quickly broke down. Before Burns was finished with them, they had admitted practically every payment they and their fellow board members had received since taking office. One of the trapped officials also provided another interesting bit of information.

"We always understood the money came from Ruef," he said, "but it was Big Jim Gallagher who passed it out."

This was important news for Burns. Just as Ruef was the only link with the major bribe payers, Board President James Gallagher, a man chiefly noted for the perpetual blank look on his face, was the only link with Ruef. Since Rudolph Spreckels, who was furnishing much of the capital for the investigation, had been asking to play some personal part in the investigation, Burns gave him the job of offering the prosecution's terms to Gallagher: the entire Board of Supervisors could either cooperate completely as state's witnesses, or face prosecution themselves on the basis of the three confessions already received.

Understandably, the supervisors balked at facing public disgrace, even as a means of escaping prison. They frantically sought some other way out, while Gallagher stalled Spreckels. The board as a whole finally took up a collection to help their confessed colleagues flee the city. Tom Lonergan, the first to try, gave up after finding a Burns operative waiting wherever he went.

"It's no use," he told Jim Gallagher plaintively.

The prime target of the squeeze play Burns had set up was, of course, Abraham Ruef. Burns fully expected that Ruef, recognizing that the testimony of his underlings would incriminate him, would try to beat them by turning state's evidence. The detective confidently awaited a private query from Ruef about the chances of a deal. But once again, Ruef did the totally unexpected. On March 4, the indicted political boss suddenly vanished.

At Heney's request, Judge Frank Dunne ordered bond revoked and Ruef taken into custody. But the county sheriff, who owed his election to Boss Ruef, blandly reported after two days that the missing man couldn't be found. Judge Dunne angrily directed the county coroner to take over the assignment. The coroner, also a Ruef man, was no more successful.

"I'll find him," Burns offered, "if the court will give me the authority."

Just three hours after his offer was accepted, the veteran detective, accompanied by his son George and several of his operatives, pushed through the door of a secluded roadhouse called the Trocadero and arrested their man. Locating Ruef had been no great problem for Burns' intelligence system. The problem lay in figuring out why the little boss, who was relaxing in an upstairs room, acted more like a fun-loving boy playing hide-and-seek than a fugitive fleeing an extortion indictment.

Judge Dunne had agreed that Ruef could be kept under guard in a hotel, since both city and county jails were run by Ruef men. "When you feel you can give me the privilege," Burns said in a mocking tone, "I'd like to sit down and have a long confidential talk with you."

Abe Ruef merely laughed, and the detective was still very much baffled. He knew his prisoner was a formidable adversary; he not only had judges who owed him favors busily attempting to take over his case, he also had cronies in the state assembly who were hurriedly promoting a special bill that would enable him to pick his own judge by demanding endless changes of venue. Why should so powerful and clever a man indulge in such senseless antics as attempting to make himself district attorney, or trying an abortive disappearing act? Why, for all his shrewdness, did Abe Ruef occasionally act as comical as he looked?

Burns' confidence had evaporated again. He felt no closer to the answer than he had been in the beginning. When he sat down for the private talk he had requested, he warily acted like an old friend who had dropped in for a social visit. Smiling delightedly, Ruef played the game with him. Both were men who did, in fact, find the art of conversation delicious. And before long, with each keeping his real thoughts to himself, they were pleasurably reminiscing about days gone by.

"When I was just starting out in the Secret Service," Burns eventually mentioned, "and earning all of three dollars a day, I once got a complaint that counterfeits were being passed from a certain tavern in St. Louis. So I walked in, ordered a drink, and gave the bartender a five-dollar bill. The bills I got back for change were all fakes, and crude ones at that. I left, walked around the block, then came back to order another drink, giving the man one of his own dollars. He held it up to the light, then gave me a mean look and tossed it back to me. 'I can't take that.' he said. 'It's counterfeit.' "

Ruef laughed with him. "That bartender was a fool. I would have accepted that bill and handed you your change like that." Ruef snapped his fingers.

Burns nodded. "Of course You're no fool. And although it helped me then, Lord deliver me from working against a fool in this case. A fool in your place right now wouldn't see that we had him all bottled up. Nothing but shaking the bars and rattling the chains would convince him. But you? You can see that we've got you. There isn't any power that can stop us. Spreckels is ready, if necessary, to spend his entire fortune on these prosecutions. We'll convict you in the French restaurant case; there isn't any finessing you can use to crawl out." He began numbering on his fingers the major bribe payers identified in his operatives' reports and the three supervisors' confessions. "We'll convict you in the United Railroads case, the Parkside Realty case, the gas company and telephone companies cases, the . . . "

"You'll never be able to convict me in all those affairs," Abe Ruef interrupted him.

"We'll prove that you received the money and that you handed it to Gallagher. But it's up to you whether you'll be pushed to the limit. You can see that you're not the man we're really after. We want to break the system. We want the fellows higher up, the corporations that corrupted the city. Now these fellows *want* us to put you away for keeps, and the public wants the same thing. It would be easy enough, and you'd make a lovely Jonah for the system."

Ruef couldn't dispute that the public was against him. Along with Fremont Older's *Bulletin* and Hearst's *Examiner,* the *Call* and the *Chronicle* had started singing for his scalp, leaving no San Francisco daily daring to defend him. But Ruef simply shrugged. It was Burns, not Ruef, who was saying the corporations were guilty, he reminded the detective; but assuming this were true, he alone could deliver them. And his price for doing so would be the dropping of all charges against him.

"That can't be done." The detective shook his head. "Not now anyway. The public wouldn't stand for it. You'll have to plead guilty in the French restaurant case. But we'll hold up sentencing indefinitely while you have a chance to prove yourself as a prosecution witness. If you come through for us, you'll be let off with a suspended sentence."

It was Ruef's turn to shake his head. Unless the indictments against him were dismissed and immunity from future prosecution promised in writing, he'd take his chances in court — as a defendant, not a state's witness.

The interview ended in this stalemate, and so did another private talk a few days later and session after session after that. Burns couldn't meet Ruef's terms for cooperation; he didn't dare trust him without at least one charge to hold over his head, and he tried in every way he knew to break the deadlock. Then the Board of Supervisors finally decided to save themselves by turning state's evidence. When, on March 24, they arrived in a body at Burns' offices in the Gladstone to answer endless questions before a battery of stenographers, the detective made sure that Board President Gallagher, the only man who could directly implicate Ruef, broke the news to Ruef in person.

"It's every man for himself now," Big Jim muttered, sullenly and defensively. "Burns has got us."

Yet even then Ruef clung to his refusal to plead guilty in the French restaurant case. Prosecutor Frank Heney was going grimly ahead, using the supervisors' confessions to win one new indictment after another against the imprisoned boss. But even the very real and increasing threat that Ruef might spend the rest of his life in San Quentin failed to break him down. His various schemes were collapsing. His friends failed to get his case taken away from Judge Dunne, or to force the bill designed to help him through the state assembly. Still, all through the month of April, Abraham Ruef clung stubbornly to his demand for total immunity.

Time was running out for Burns. Testimony was scheduled to begin in Ruef's trial by May 15, and unless the detective could talk the man into becoming a prosecution witness by then, all hope of indicting the so-called higher-ups would be lost. But as thorough as the investigation had been, as often as Burns had talked to, studied, and matched wits with the prisoner, he had found no way to bring Ruef and the vital testimony he could provide over to his side.

The man was a puzzle in small ways as well as large. Why, for example, was Ruef so unreasonably fastidious? Why did such a homely, unprepossessing little character use three separate mirrors simultaneously to pass judgment on a haircut after having a private barber in? Why did a man so narrow-shouldered and pudgy have his tailors rework every stitch of his suits to perfection? And why, instead of shunning reporters as he should have been doing, did he welcome them eagerly and search the papers regularly for his name and picture? Extreme vanity, an almost childlike love of publicity — these were certainly strange qualities to find in a shrewd, behind-the-scenes political boss.

Or were they? Could vanity in itself be the answer, overlooked in its profound simplicity, make understanding and breaking him more of a problem of psychology than deductive logic?

Was Ruef really happy in his backstage role? Or did he secretly envy the public figures he manipulated — the handsome, distinguished-looking incompetents like Mayor Schmitz, whom Ruef could put into offices he himself couldn't hold because of his unimpressive figure and unattractive looks? Was it really just power and profit Ruef craved? Or was it the thrill of living vicariously through the puppets he had installed? Could it be that secondhand public attention no longer satisfied Ruef? Was this the reason for the recent foolhardy but headline-making stunts he'd pulled? Beneath all the complex and polished facets of his personality, could it be that this behind-the-scenes political boss was essentially a frustrated would-be celebrity?

Burns had little to lose by acting on this sudden notion. He had already exhausted every other approach. With less than a week left, he began concentrating solely on cultivating Ruef's vanity.

"If you *did* plead guilty in that French restaurant case, it would be a sensation," he said to Ruef one day.

"Why?" Ruef wondered aloud. The usual method of

entering a new plea, he reminded Burns, consisted of nothing more sensational than handing a petition to a court clerk.

"Yes, but why do it that way? Why not keep everyone in the dark until you're scheduled to take the stand? Think of it. The courtroom will be crowded. I'll play innocent, of course, until you actually make your statement, and what a statement that can be. You could pull out all the stops, make yourself a sympathetic figure and give facts that will move the whole room to tears — the whole city, in fact, because the newspapers will get it from the stenographer and run it word for word. The effect will be increased because this is the last thing anyone will be expecting you to do."

A bored look remained on Ruef's face, and an indifferent tone stayed in his voice. But there was an almost imperceptible change in his manner, and try as he might he couldn't help revealing a flicker of interest. Certain he saw his opening, Burns bore in relentlessly. From that time on, instead of painting grim descriptions of prison life, Burns spoke of little else but the spectacular scene a surprise change of plea would create, the headlines and the photo-filled front pages that would follow.

He had moments of doubt, of course, talks with Ruef when he felt ridiculous in attempting to sway so clever a man with such a childish, emotional approach. And Abraham Ruef remained noncommittal to the end. Even when he took the stand in court and asked the judge's permission to make a statement, he still seemed to be delighting in mystifying everyone, Burns included.

Ruef spoke at length about his spotless early career and his good intentions. He rambled on and on, and the closest he came to any admission of wrongdoing was to say that "a desire to hold together a political organization built up with much effort" had influenced him "to lower the high ideals" for which he had allegedly "hitherto striven." He even went so far as to claim he was "innocent of the offense charged in this indictment." But in the end, sounding somewhat like a talking-machine record running down, he asked "to withdraw the plea heretofore submitted and enter the contrary plea."

Judge Dunne was as puzzled as everyone else. "What *is* your plea then?" he asked.

There was a long, heavy stretch of silence. "Guilty," Abraham Ruef finally whispered.

In the uproar that followed, prosecutor Heney turned in amazement to the detective beside him, as Older and Spreckels pushed through the crowd to join them.

"Why didn't you tell us you had him talked into changing his plea?" all three wanted to know.

"Because until he actually got his mouth around that word 'guilty,'" Burns admitted, "I wasn't halfway sure he'd go through with it."

William J. Burns was being interviewed regularly through that summer of 1907, by magazine writers as well as newspapermen. "I'm not asking any game," he told one of them, "harder than the one I played with Ruef."

But actually, Burns and Heney were asking for a far harder game. Just ten days after the political boss made his surprise change of plea in court, they were using the information he gave to proceed as planned against the "big guns" who were their ultimate objectives — the bribe-paying corporations. Grand jury indictments were obtained against fully a dozen utility officials and realty promoters, including, most significantly, President Patrick Calhoun and Chief Counsel Tirey Ford of the powerful United Railroads combine.

A man of great prestige and wealth, Patrick Calhoun felt above the law. He had never really believed that the moral crusade his fellow millionaire, Rudolph Spreckels, was financing would be carried beyond the corrupted to the corrupters. In fact, Calhoun had taken quick advantage of the breakdown in city government resulting from Burns' expose of the bribe-taking Union-Labor Party officials. Importing armed hoodlums, he fought and won a labor war that smashed the local trolley-workers' union at a cost of more than $1,000,000, some 250 injured, and four men killed. Finding himself and several of his subordinates indicted like common felons on May 25, Calhoun's rage was explosive and ominous.

Instead of disbanding the armed force he had used to destroy the union, he now increased it to what the San Francisco *Examiner* called "the proportions of a small army," composed of what the *Call,* in turn, described as "a motley train of gunfighters, pug-uglies, disreputable detectives, thugs and women of the half-world," with a "wolfish pack of gutter journalists" to handle public relations. Heading the "retinue of the trolley magnates" was a prominent detective and political figure from Los Angeles, a tough, tricky character named Luther Brown. And heading the high-priced legal team that was assembled to defend the indicted United Railroads officials in court — reportedly retained for the highest single fee ever paid an American attorney — was a friend of Brown's who was even more prominent, the famed and colorful Earl Rogers.

Rogers was a tall, elegantly dressed man who frequently seemed more an actor than an attorney in court. His private life was a shambles. He was a hopeless alcoholic and a notorious woman chaser. Permanently and deeply in debt no matter how much he earned, he held the uncontested title among bill collectors of being the West's worst deadbeat. But he was also a brilliant lawyer. His record in the courtroom spoke for itself: no one had successfully defended more men of high position against everything from vice and morals charges through murder trials.

Interestingly enough, from the moment he arrived in San Francisco that summer, Earl Rogers shrugged off his courtroom opponent Frank Heney. With the instinctive antagonism of one colorful figure for another, Rogers made it clear that he regarded William J. Burns as his real adversary.

"Way down in his gumshoe soul," the attorney boasted, "Burns knows I'm going to beat him."

He also made it clear that he had no intention of wait-

141

ing until court convened to begin winning the case. He had been on a first-name basis with Abraham Ruef for years, and there was no legal way he could be kept from visiting the imprisoned star witness, who had so far cooperated with the prosecution in convicting former Mayor Schmitz of extortion. During their meetings, he kept insisting to Ruef that Heney was not to be trusted.

It was a clever tactic. Ruef had not had many dealings with the prosecutor. The commitments had all been made by Burns. Rogers soon had Ruef wondering if the prosecutor could be counted upon to keep the detective's promise of a suspended sentence in return for his testimony. From there, it was just a small step to start Ruef wondering if it wouldn't be better to cast his lot with the impressive United Railroads forces.

"Trust Rogers instead of Heney," Burns would counterattack when he saw the prisoner, "and you'll go to San Quentin for ten to fifteen years." But Burns could see Ruef wavering as the show of strength by the trolley magnates' retinue became steadily more impressive. By the time the trial of United Railroads Chief Counsel Tirey Ford opened in September, the prosecution was no longer certain Ruef should even be called to the stand.

Moreover, another new element had been added to the game. A surprisingly large number of the state's most notorious thugs seemed to have taken an interest in the proceedings against Tirey Ford. "Your honor," Frank Heney protested to the presiging judge, William P. Lawlor, "I have noticed about half a dozen of the most desperate characters in California, including Dave Nagle and Bogie O'Donnell and the Banjo-eyed Kid . . . sitting in this courtroom, in close proximity to the jury. They were here the first morning of this trial, they have been here ever since, and they are in the employ of the United Railroads."

Bill Burns had guarded jurors and witnesses from desperate characters before. But United Railroads detective chief

Luther Brown was an imaginative adversary. A magazine writer named Walter Dorland had arrived in San Francisco at the same time as Brown and Rogers. Dorland immediately sought out Tom Lonergan, the former supervisor who had been the first man bribed at the Dreamland Rink. Saying that he hoped to get an exclusive story, Dorland entertained Lonergan and his wife lavishly, taking them to the most expensive restaurants. A check by Burns revealed that Dorland was a United Railroads employee who had never written a published word in his life. Burns warned Lonergan to call him whenever approached by the man.

On the evening of October 22, Lonergan reported that Dorland had just phoned him, suggesting they leave Mrs. Lonergan at home for once and "make a night of it" with "a couple of nice girls."

Fear overcame temptation and the former supervisor dutifully notified Burns. "What should I do?" he asked.

"Go out and meet him," Burns suggested, "but have your wife along. Play dumb. Whatever you do, don't get in his car." Burns was parked near Lonergan's home when Dorland arrived, and watched as Dorland, seeing Lonergan's wife, drove off again in disgust, taking the two ladies he had procured with him. But another car also drove off from a parking spot in the shadows. In it were Luther Brown, the Banjo-eyed Kid, and several accomplices. The promised night with the nice girls, Burns' men who had infiltrated the United Railroads' organization later insisted, would have been Lonergan's last.

Burns deliberately kept word of this abduction attempt from Frank Heney. He didn't want Heney to bring it into the open yet. Matching theatrics with theatrics, Burns preferred that defense attorney Earl Rogers fall into a trap of the same kind Rogers himself was famous for springing. As hoped, Rogers spent the entire next morning of the Ford trial using Walter Dorland's notes and manuscript in an attempt to ridicule Tom Lonergan's previous testimony. Not until afternoon was Heney given Burns' report so that he could reveal, on redirect examination, the kidnapping plan with which the defense by implication had associated itself. The news was a sensation that sent courtroom reporters racing for the corridors, and Earl Rogers could only angrily protest that he knew absolutely nothing about what had happened the night before.

The famous defense attorney stared for a long time at the stocky, redhaired detective. And for all the years William J. Burns had spent chasing and cornering criminals he would say then and later that he had never seen a look of more vehement hatred.

It was soon obvious that, if Earl Rogers had honestly known nothing of the plot to eliminate Lonergan, he had very little control over his friend and constant companion Luther Brown. Just four days later, Fremont Older received a call from a "Mr. Stapleton" who was supposedly waiting at the Savoy Hotel with "some very important information." Since it was broad daylight, the *Bulletin* editor didn't inform Burns, and set out alone. On busy Van Ness Avenue, he was forced at gunpoint into an automobile by Brown and three others, taken south to Redwood City, held until dark there, then secretly taken aboard a train bound for Los Angeles.

Fortunately for Older, his abductors were a little too talkative in the dining car. A passenger heard enough to suspect that a kidnapping was taking place. He slipped off the train at Salinas to make a long distance call. Burns and Heney spent the rest of the night making hurried calls of their own. A sheriff and his deputies were waiting when the train rolled into Santa Barbara the next morning. And the men who had carted Older off as a prisoner were returned to San Francisco in the same manner.

Luther Brown had a clever cover story ready. An earlier typographical error in the *Bulletin* had confused him with one of his own men, a J.C. Brown, giving him a pretext for claiming that he'd been libelled. From an old friend in Los Angeles who happened to be a justice of the peace, Luther Brown had obtained a warrant for Older's arrest, and he'd found two more old friends who happened to be Los Angeles area constables to help him carry off the newsman.

But Burns' informants in the United Railroads' camp reported Older had been scheduled to be "shot while attempting to escape" in the hills beyond Santa Barbara. And San Francisco took such a dim view of Los Angeles' unique and unrequested assistance in dispensing justice that the two constables needed an armed escort of Burns' men in order to leave town safely. Luther Brown was promptly indicted for kidnapping.

The incident had a particularly ominous overtone for William J. Burns. He had his entire family with him now, for the first time in his career except for brief visits. And the Van Ness Avenue from which Older had been abducted was the same street that fronted St. Brigid's, the school that his 11-year-old daughter Kathleen was attending.

Annie Ressler Burns had come west that spring to stay for a time with her husband and her sons George and Raymond. She returned to Ohio just long enough to watch her older daughter Florence graduate from the Columbus School for Girls, then sold the family house and moved to San Francisco. But there was a price to be paid for having her husband and all her children together at last. Prosecutor Frank Heney angrily told the court, "There are at the present time following William J. Burns and myself about this city armed thugs in the employ of Patrick Calhoun . . . They have besieged the courtroom, followed us in automobiles and shadowed our homes."

Annie Burns had full trust in the guards her husband posted about the house she had rented on Clay Street. But she was subjected to so many threatening notes and phone calls that she quietly moved to a house on Nob Hill, then another on Jones Street, then still others in a total of seven moves in just two years.

Florence Burns, at 19, could understand the necessity of having her steps dogged by a bodyguard, and even the necessity of having the young men who came calling questioned and searched, although this wasn't exactly advantageous to her social life. But these were tortured times for little Kathleen, who found herself escorted to and from school and even watched on the playground by a hulking Burns man. Her classmates teased her about the ever-present bodyguard, and once she bitterly turned on the detective, hitting him with her small fists and tearfully asking him to leave her alone.

One day the father of another girl at St. Brigid's invited Kathy to join a number of children he was taking on an outing to the mountains. Understandably excited about the invitation, she was furious with her own father when he refused to let her go. But the gentleman who had issued the invitation, by coincidence or otherwise, had been seen visiting the United Railroads office on several occasions.

There was another reason why Kathy's San Francisco stay was hardly the most fondly remembered period of her life. She had the dubious pleasure, every morning, of seeing her father in the funny papers.

William Randolph Hearst had turned against the graft prosecution, reportedly because he hadn't been allowed to pick Mayor Schmitz' replacement when San Francisco voters threw out the discredited Union-Labor government. With the added enthusiasm that apostasy often brings, he soon had his *Examiner* attempting to outdo the United Railroads' own "gutter journalists" in ridiculing the men he had so recently been praising. Hearst had hired a bright young cartoonist named Bud Fisher, who had created a new comic-strip character named Colonel A. Mutt. Mutt was a tall, ungainly figure who would eventually share his strip with a short fellow named Jeff and become an enduring national institution. But in the beginning, Colonel Mutt's companions for his daily adventures in the *Examiner* — so thinly disguised that no one could possibly mistake them — were the principal figures in the anti-graft campaign.

Heney had become "Beany," a big-headed freak of a dwarf wearing a little cap above a cross-eyed idiot grin. Spreckles was "Pickles." Older, possibly because of some obscure ethic concerning a fellow journalist, was left unsatirized, but Judges Lawlor and Dunne were Judges "Crawler" and "Finished" respectively. And in a play on his name, red hair and brisk, peppery nature, William J. Burns was "Hot Tobasco Burns." Sometimes Fisher would picture Burns in ridiculous situations — drawing him, for example, as a chorus girl doing an absurd vaudeville dance with Beany — and further billing him as "The Greatest Special Detective That Ever Did Special Detecting."

It infuriated Kathleen when her father laughed at this mockery and even entertained Bud Fisher in his home on occasion. But the comic strip was undeniably funny. On the campuses of the state, as Florence noticed when she began attending the University of California, youthful idealists were adopting one of Fisher's creations to proclaim their support of the graft clean-up. They put on "Beany" caps, and college students have been wearing them ever since.

There was another young man sketching courtroom scenes through that year of 1908, a more serious art student named Randal Borough working for the San Francisco *Call* . Borough was destined to become one of the nation's leading commercial artists. Although William J. Burns, whom he often depicted, scarcely noticed him, and Florence Burns never met him at the time, he was destined to become, some seven years later, the famous detective's first son-in-law.

As protective as Mr. Burns may have been where his daughters were concerned, no one could ever accuse him of babying his boys. Instead of being given a bodyguard, Sherman Burns, just sixteen when he arrived in San Francisco, was given a revolver. Each afternoon that first fall, after finishing a prep football practice at Lowell High School, he would shed his uniform and equipment, get into his street clothes and his shoulder holster, and report for work as one of Abraham Ruef's guards.

Unlike both his slim older brothers, Sherman was as broad-shouldered and stocky as his father — a fact that the senior Burns put to good use when he wanted to shake the United Railroads detectives who were invariably following him. Father and son would simply switch hats and overcoats in the back seat of an automobile. The driver would slow down for a moment. Sherman then would leap out and go sprinting down the sidewalk, usually with a panting, pursuing carload of Patrick Calhoun's men hot at his heels.

One evening in the spring of 1908, when Sherman was alone at the Burns office, he got a call from a man named Cohn. The prosecution had given up all hope of using Abe Ruef as a witness by then. Earl Rogers had won his struggle for Ruef's allegiance, and prosecutor Heney had no choice but to bring Ruef himself to trial. Mr. Cohn was claiming, on the phone, to have "some important information about the Ruef case." He gave an address and asked that one of Burns' men meet him there.

Sherman's father was out of town at the time, as were both his brothers. The boy knew this was exactly the same kind of invitation that had led editor Fremont Older into a close escape from assassination, but Cohn had sounded sincere to Sherman, and he decided to check the tip out.

The address turned out to be a cheap variety store. Cohn was a part-time tailor who lived upstairs. He led young Burns up to his apartment and, with a worried glance around to make sure he wasn't overheard, whispered his information.

"There's a man on the Ruef jury named Morris Haas who has a criminal record. He was in prison back in Philadelphia for embezzlement."

Sherman was familiar with the reports on jurors that his father's men had made. Haas was a whiskey salesman and a question mark on the prosecution list because of a reputation for consuming too much of his own stock. But he had no known police history.

"We've checked him out, and his record is clear," Sherman said.

"He's changed his name," the tailor asserted. "He had a different name then."

This was possible. Sherman stared at the informant for a moment, then asked the question he knew his father would have asked. "Why are you telling us this?"

"Because he's been too friendly with my wife," Cohn said, his voice rising in anger. "He keeps telling her she's the woman he should have married, and . . . "

Just then Mrs. Cohn walked in, and her husband had no more to say. But he'd said enough. Sherman hurried out to Frank Heney's house and told him the story. A telegraphed query to authorities in Pennsylvania brought both a confirmation and a rogue's gallery photo of the man now calling himself Morris Haas.

Several days later, prosecutor Heney challenged juror Haas by asking him again whether or not he knew of anything that could disqualify him from jury duty. Haas shook his head. Even when he was specifically reminded that a felony conviction would be considered disqualifying by the court, Morris Haas stubbornly attempted to bluff his way onto the jury. Heney had to confront him with his photograph to get him dismissed.

Haas left the courtroom nursing a grievance that clearly involved more than public disgrace. To his friend, Mrs. Miriam Cohn, he mysteriously mentioned that "Heney did me out of $4,000." And to the patrons of several taverns on his whiskey sales route, he muttered that he intended to get even.

The prosecution had more important worries by then. All the willfulness and obstinacy of Spreckels, Older, Heney, and Burns couldn't change the fact that the tide had turned against them. The California Court of Appeals had set aside Schmitz' conviction on a technicality; and without Ruef's testimony, there was little purpose in trying the former mayor again. Ruef's defection had already caused successive trials of United Railroads counsel Tirey Ford to end first with a hung jury and then with an acquittal, and the chances of convicting Calhoun and the other indicted corporation and utility officials seemed no brighter. For that matter, a jury had been unable to agree on a verdict in the Ruef trial.

Furthermore, public support was giving way to apathy after almost two years of headlines. To most San Franciscans, the graft investigation had already accomplished its purpose. A corrupt government had been exposed and ousted, and this seemed enough. The belief of Burns and Heney that a graft system would re-establish itself immediately unless the bribe-payers were also exposed and punished was far ahead of its time. To a great many citizens, the complex prolonging of the crusade editor Older had started seemed senseless.

Public apathy afforded a fertile climate for Patrick Calhoun's publicity campaign against the probe. United Railroads and its ally, the Southern Pacific, had started a new San Francisco daily, the *Globe,* purchased the weekly *Mission Times* outright, and subsidized such sheets as the Fresno *Herald* and the Sacramento *Union.* Still other newspapers were being paid for vilifying the prosecution on a straight space-rate basis. Harrison Gray Otis, the elderly owner of the Los Angeles *Times,* once boasted that he had received $15,000 for running attacks on Burns and Heney that he would have been happy to print for nothing.

Burns had more dangerous attacks than those made editorially to worry about as he kept an endless watch over witnesses and jurors. With Ruef's change of heart, the testimony of Jim Gallagher, the former Board of Supervisors president and the man who had distributed the graft payments Ruef had received, became all-important. On April 21, 1908, a bomb went off in Gallagher's apartment, shattering all the furniture in a room he had just left. Later, another explosion blasted some rental flats he was building. Ordinarily, Gallagher would have been there at the time to pay his carpenters their wages. Luckily, rain had delayed him that day.

Despite this terrorism, Burns continued to notch some victories of his own. By mid-July, he had a confession from a United Railroads laborer named John Claudianes, who admitted that he and his brother Peter had been hired by a United Railroads foreman named Felix Paduveris to assassinate not only Gallagher but also Burns, Heney, Older, and Spreckels. John had backed out of the scheme. Peter had made the two unsuccessful attempts on Gallagher's life alone, then fled.

Burns' oldest son George was given the assignment of going after the missing Claudianes brother. He tracked Peter Claudianes to Reno, lost him there, scoured half the country for a time, then finally closed in to make an arrest in Chicago. Brought back to the coast in handcuffs, Claudianes was quickly tried and sentenced to life imprisonment. But there was no chance of reaching the men who had paid for his efforts. Felix Paduveris, the foreman who had done the immediate hiring, had been rushed out of the country, reportedly to Europe.

In the course of the long search for Claudianes, George Burns received an offer to go east and undertake a private investigation on his own. Since the salary would be high and the San Francisco prosecutions seemed to offer little more than routine duty at the moment, he decided to accept the offer. He discussed the exact nature of the job with no one, but his mother was deeply worried. She'd noticed that George had picked up on that trackdown a persistent cough for which, even in the California autumn, there seemed to be no cure. Despite her objections, George was soon off for the snow and cold of Minneapolis. Then he spent some weeks in chilly Indianapolis. By mid-November, he was in his home town of Columbus, where he suddenly collapsed and was taken to a hospital. Appendicitis proved to be a minor part of the problem; when he was finally able to return to the West coast, he went directly to St. Helena Sanitarium. He had tuberculosis.

In his absence, ironically enough, there had been no lack of excitement in San Francisco.

The Friday morning of November 13, 1908, had seemed, except perhaps to the superstitious, no different from any other day of the long-drawn-out anti-graft campaign. For the Burns family at breakfast, the varsity football game Sherman would be playing for Lowell was the major event of the hours ahead. Bill Burns had some work waiting in the district attorney's office, and he asked Raymond to take his place beside Frank Heney in court, where the prosecutor was making his third attempt to convict Abraham Ruef after being stymied by two hung juries.

Most other San Francisco families had long been finding Bud Fisher's cartoons in the morning *Examiner* more interesting than any newspaper account of the endless courtroom activity. One of the *Examiner's* recent offerings hadn't seemed too humorous, though — a picture of Beany with an "X" lettered on his throat and a caption reading, "X Marks the Spot"

Big Jim Gallagher, the survivor of the two dynamiting attempts, was on the stand for most of that day, retelling the story that had once made headlines but could dull the senses of any courtroom audience now. In the late-afternoon drowsiness, Judge Lawlor ordered a brief recess. All of the principals took the opportunity to stretch their legs. Even Abe Ruef stepped outside for a cigarette.

A uniformed policeman was on duty at the door. Frank Heney's assigned bodyguard, John Foley, remained in court along with 22-year-old Raymond Burns. The near-empty room seemed chilly during the recess, and Foley had just gone over to stir up the fire in the stove when the crowd started streaming back. Heney was one of the first to return, sitting down again at the counsel table and chatting with a prosecution clerk.

The officer at the door saw no reason to stop a man in a dark overcoat who walked in with the rest of the audience and moved down the aisle in a normal fashion. No one present but the prosecutor, whose back was turned, even knew the man. But Morris Haas, the ex-convict who had been dismissed from the first Ruef jury, was back in court. And he suddenly pulled a revolver from his coat pocket and fired at Frank Heney's head.

With half the confused and frightened crowd still standing, there was no chance for Raymond Burns and John Foley to do any shooting. Both sprinted and shoved their way through the mass of people and leaped for the gunman, crashing into him before he could get off a second shot. Wrestling him to the floor, they smashed the pistol out of his hand. He managed to break free and got as far as a corner of the jury box before they caught him again, slamming him down and handcuffing his hands behind him.

Heney was slumped across the table with his face in his hands and blood flooding out through his fingers. The bullet had entered the right side of his jaw and passed through to lodge in the lower left side of his neck. A doctor from the audience made an examination and then whispered to the judge that the prosecutor had no chance whatever to live. Lawlor ordered the court clerk to take a "dying statement" from Heney before an ambulance rushed him the few blocks to Central Emergency Hospital. By that time, William J. Burns was on the scene.

"Who paid you to do this?" he shouted at the man his son and Foley were guarding.

Morris Haas sobbed that he hadn't been paid. Burns didn't believe him, but he didn't have time to ask any more questions. A furious mob that would number more than one thousand within an hour of the shooting already was massing outside the courtroom. The public mood had changed abruptly. Fearful of a lynching, Burns rushed Haas to the County Jail.

By evening, with Central Emergency reporting Heney's condition as critical, more mobs were forming. The San Francisco *Examiner* had to barricade its building and pass out rifles and shotguns to its printers when citizens who remembered the "X" mark on Beany's throat jammed the streets outside, threatening a return to vigilante days. When Frank Heney was transferred to Lane Hospital that night, several hundred waiting well-wishers unhitched the horses and drew the ambulance themselves to make the ride over the cobblestones smoother and less painful. It remained finally for Bill Burns, emerging from the hospital after a night at the prosecutor's side, to give the crowds their first firm word of hope:

"Frank is going to make it. You folks know what a lawyer's jaw muscles are."

But the indignation that had flamed in the city that night was spreading. The *Examiner* tried to make hurried amends by rushing out an extra that praised Heney's courage and offering pious prayers for his recovery, and practically all California newspapers but those owned outright by United Railroads and the Southern Pacific felt compelled to do the same. The Los Angeles *Times,* published a safe distance from San Francisco, was an exception. Though callous, its candor was almost refreshing at this moment of general hypocrisy. "Well or ill, whole or wounded, we cannot modify in one jot our opinion of this man," asserted Harrison Gray Otis. "We regret the elimination of Heney out of the case in the way in which it was done. But desirous of the good name of the state and the peace of San Francisco . . . we cannot help rejoicing."

Still, the labor-hating Otis, who had backed Burns and Heney wholeheartedly when they were exposing only petty Union-Labor Party men, was almost alone in his public rejoicing. Expressions of outrage and sympathy were coming in from all over the country. INEXPRESSIBLY SHOCKED, President Roosevelt wired. THE INFAMOUS CHARACTER OF THE WOULD-BE ASSASSIN NO LESS THAN THE INFAMOUS CHARACTER OF THE DEED CALL ATTENTION IN A STRIKING WAY TO THE TRUE CHAR-ACTER OF THE FORCES AGAINST WHICH MR. HENEY AND YOU AND YOUR ASSOCIATES HAVE BEEN FIGHTING.

Burns was busily trying to learn more about the character of those forces from the man who had shot Heney. To his amazement, the city police chief refused to let him question the prisoner. The detective had to get a court order before he could see Morris Haas and even then was allowed only an hour. He won an admission that Haas had been urged on by "several persons whose names I won't tell you." But before Burns could get another court order and make further attempts to learn those names, Morris Haas was found dead in his cell with a new pistol beside him and a bullet hole in his forehead.

Haas' sudden, bloody exit was as much of a sensation as his attempt to kill Frank Heney had been. And if Burns had any remaining doubts about the opposition's readiness to take any steps to protect itself, and its ability to cover those steps, the next series of events erased them.

Although there were no powder burns on the dead man's skin, and though Raymond Burns, John Foley and two police-men had searched Haas thoroughly and swore that he had no second pistol concealed when he entered the jail, a coroner's jury officially labelled the death a suicide. Moreover, the police chief who had refused to allow Burns to question Haas acted strangely troubled for two weeks, then died a myster-ious death himself. Another coroner's jury called it an accidental drowning, although the man was well known to be a strong swimmer.

With two key witnesses rendered mute, Burns' efforts to find out who instigated the attempted murder of Heney had come to the same futile end as this attempt to reach the men who had hired the Claudianes brothers. He turned grimly back to the prosecution of Abraham Ruef. Immediately after the shooting, public feeling had flared so intensely that one of the city's most prominent attorneys, Hiram Johnson, openly called for a lynching. "There is no use going on trying this rat three or four times more," he had shouted at a public meeting. Once Johnson cooled off, he decided on another procedure. Along with several other leading lawyers, he volunteered to carry on with the trial in place of the stricken prosecutor.

Johnson did a masterful job. In fact, for all of Burns' affection for his wounded friend, he had to admit that Johnson was more effective in presenting the case against Ruef. Five steady years of prosecutions, in Oregon and California had left Heney's nerve ends too raw, his rage too easily triggered. "I don't mind Heney," attorney Earl Rogers had once laughed. "That temper of his lets me lead him around like a bear by the nose." But no one was leading his fresh replacement around. And on December 10, Frank Heney himself showed up in court to hear a jury bring in a verdict of guilty against Abraham Ruef.

Heney publicly thanked Johnson for so ably replacing him, then told a cheering crowd that he was ready to return to action. The next man to go to jail, he promised, would be Patrick Calhoun.

All through the first half of the year 1909, Frank Heney fought to keep that promise and put the United Railroads president in prison. Though the special prosecutor had been left partially deafened, and pain shot through his neck and jaw with every word he spoke, he pitted himself against the entire legal team the gifted Earl Rogers headed. There were no further murder attempts, but for a moment it looked as if the long-delayed showdown would be a gun battle in the best tradition of the Old West. On March 27, Bill Burns arrested one of his own clerks for selling prosecution papers

156

to the defense. And with a warrant in his pocket, he then staged a surprise raid on the United Railroads offices.

Pushing the red-faced, sputtering Calhoun aside, Burns ordered files and safes broken open. Some seven hundred stolen reports, most of them hidden in the private safe of the company's president, were systematically identified. Trolley company detectives hurriedly rounded up a gang of toughs. When Burns led his men out of the building, leaving the cluttered wreckage of an office behind, the Calhoun forces were waiting. Burns' men had their guns drawn, and their chief was obviously prepared to let them use them. The prospective shoot-down turned out to be a stare-down. The streetcar gang, including such characters as Butch Bell, Kid Nelson and Bunco Kelly, stepped aside.

The prosecution had some good moments in court, too, through that final campaign of a three-year struggle. Charging that Calhoun was being persecuted by a business competitor, defense attorney Rogers kept insinuating that the municipal trolley system Rudolph Spreckels and others had once offered to construct without profit was a "rival street railway." Rogers repeatedly dared Heney to put Spreckels on the stand. Suddenly the prosecutor not only accepted the challenge but offered in evidence a detailed listing of every cent Spreckels had spent in financing the graft clean-up. Then he dared the defense to do the same.

"I beg your pardon?" Rogers was caught off guard.

"I say," Heney repeated, "will you produce an itemized account of monies expended in opposition to these prosecutions?"

Earl Rogers found himself staring at the confident grin of William J. Burns, who was waiting with a thick pile of signed statements from discarded thugs, confessed jury bribers and even the Claudianes brothers — all testifying to money received from United Railroads sources. This might have been admissable as evidence if the defense had opened the door by making any pretense of matching the prosecution's financial disclosures. Instead, Rogers quickly backed away. With a great show of indignation, he declared such disclosures outside the jurisdiction of the trial.

Still, the public fervor roused by Heney's shooting had already ebbed again. When another court failed to convict Rogers' crony Luther Brown for the kidnapping of editor Fremont Older, most California newspapers heatedly condemmed the verdict; but several suggested the jury had merely reflected the general boredom with the entire, seemingly interminable affair. Furthermore, without the testimony of Abraham Ruef, the prosecution lacked the solid evidence it needed to convict Calhoun. Tirey Ford, who had distributed the $200,000, already had been acquitted; and Patrick Calhoun, who ordered the graft payments, was one step further removed from the actual criminal acts.

The former supervisors could be paraded before the jury to tell of receiving $4,000 apiece for approving the United Railroads franchise. United States Mint officials could be brought in to testify about Calhoun's instructions to release the money to Ford. But the chain of evidence linking Calhoun to the payments, as Earl Rogers ably pointed out, was both circumstantial and incomplete. On June 15, still another deadlocked jury was dismissed.

By then, William J. Burns was almost beyond caring. His son George had appeared to be recovering for a time at St. Helena, but he suffered a severe relapse and was rushed down to a hospital at Morovia. On May 25, 1909, George Edward Burns died from tuberculosis. His father was left temporarily crippled in his work — dull-eyed, silent, thoroughly sick of San Francisco.

The war that four men had waged against a city's corruption was over, although tag ends sputtered for a time. Frank Heney was determined to try Calhoun again, and he ran for district attorney that fall. But he was defeated, and he retired to private practice, exhausted, deafened, and scarred. He had made many enemies, he was only moderately successful as a lawyer, and little was publicly heard of him again.

Rudolph Spreckels paid the bills to the end without protest — a total of nearly $250,000. For whatever consolation it may have been, the men he had fought had spent millions. More than once, in private conversation, Spreckels echoed the estimate the San Francisco *Call* made of the graft fighters' efforts:

"They tried to do too much, too fast."

But more had been done than was apparent at the moment. The air had been cleared and the system of graft laid bare for all California. The crest of popularity attorney Hiram Johnson had gained by substituting for the wounded Heney swept him into the governor's office. Long before Johnson went on to the U.S. Senate and national prominence, Rudolph Spreckels' original ambition had been realized: the Southern Pacific's domination of state government had been broken.

The prolonged graft investigation had other interesting aftermaths. On March 7, 1911 — after exhausting every avenue of appeal and receiving no help whatsoever from the United Railroads or Earl Rogers once Patrick Calhoun was out of danger — Abraham Ruef entered San Quentin to begin a 14-year sentence. Arguing that Ruef no longer was a danger to anyone, and that he was the wrong man to be serving this long a term, Fremont Older, the crusading editor who had set off the investigation in the first place, immediately launched a new crusade — a campaign to have Ruef paroled. His best efforts were unsuccessful this time.

By then, William J. Burns was concentrating his full attention and all his bristling energy on another headline-making chase. In an earlier bit of irony, he had answered a call indirectly emanating from the very newspaper that had been the most savage in attacking him, the only major newspaper that had publicly rejoiced when Frank Heney lay wounded. On October 1, 1910, in an act of mass murder that shocked the entire nation, someone had dynamited the Los Angeles *Times* building.

PART FIVE

Burns and His Bloodhounds

At about 5:45 P.M. on September 30, 1910, a slim, gaunt-faced man furtively carried a suitcase into "Ink Alley," a shadowy passageway where the materials used to print the Los Angeles *Times* were delivered. Emerging empty-handed a moment later, he hurried away.

At a few minutes past 1:00 A.M., with about one hundred employees hard at work on the morning edition, the sound of the presses was suddenly blotted out by a blast that shook the entire massive stone structure. Stunned and deafened, those inside saw the whole south wall on the Broadway Street side become honeycombed with cracks and begin crumbling. All at once, the second floor gave way beneath the weight of the linotypes. The huge machines crashed down on the office staff below, and continued on through to shatter the heating plant and the big gas mains in the basement. Flames roared up through floor boards that had splintered like kindling, and the three-story building was soon a huge torch lighting up the sky.

The surrounding streets were jammed within minutes. The city's night people poured forth from taverns and restaurants; others who had been asleep emerged half-dressed from hotels. They stood by horrified and helpless. The terrible

160

searing heat stopped them from coming close, yet the sheer spectacle and the shrieks of the trapped victims made it impossible to turn away. Twisted faces appeared at the windows — young copy boys, elderly scrubwomen, reporters, printers, editors, typesetters. They stared at the street below, then could be seen looking back at the bright flames and dark smoke. The ones who decided to jump lay writhing and screaming or unconscious or dead on the concrete. Fire engines clanged up, but water hoses were of little use against the gas-fed flame. Heroic firemen, policemen and volunteers had their hands burned raw keeping ladders tight to the building. Those who managed to climb up were singed by the fire and choked by the smoke. All night long the crippled, the disfigured and the dead were carried off.

By late morning, with the wreckage still smoldering and the smell of burnt flesh sharp and sickening in the air, the nation's most famous detective was on the scene, hastily hired by the City of Los Angeles. And strangely enough, William J. Burns soon became certain that he had already started this investigation — that he had been working on it, in fact, nearly a month before the explosion occurred.

Burns had been busy in the fifteen months that had gone by since the close of the San Francisco graft case. Now well into middle age, he realized that his talent and reputation promised far greater rewards than he could ever get as a U.S. agent. He had no intention of letting the team of picked men he'd built up through six years on special federal assignment disintegrate. Moving his family to Chicago, he left government service and allied his land-frauds and graft-case veterans with an established private detective organization headed by a man named William P. Sheridan. Formally born in September of 1909, the Burns & Sheridan Detective Agency had publicly proclaimed a policy of accepting neither divorce nor strikebreaking cases.

Since staging adultery evidence for divorces was the bread-

and-butter business of the small detective agencies of the era, while the supplying of strikebreakers was the mainstay of the giants of the field, Burns' obsession with respectability brought cynical chuckles from his competitors. But just three months later, his fledgling firm pulled off an astonishing coup. He took the most sought-after plum in the profession, the American Bankers Association contract for the protection of its 11,000 member banks, away from the gigantic rival that had held it for fifteen years, the infinitely powerful Pinkerton Agency.

This was front-page news. The Pinkertons accused Burns of underbidding their rates, and Burns answered with a straight-faced promise not to infringe on the Pinkerton-dominated field of racetrack protection. But to fulfill his contract, and similar agreements that followed with the National Retail Dry Goods Association and with various chains of hotels, Burns had to expand his firm almost overnight into an organization that could rival the Pinkerton Agency in more substantial ways than glib press releases. For several winter months, his life was a dizzying rush of train rides.

Dazed by the pace, William Sheridan sold out his interest just a few months after the partnership was incorporated. By March 11, 1910, when the firm became the William J. Burns National Detective Agency, with its namesake as president and his son Raymond as both secretary-treasurer and manager of the Chicago headquarters, a network of some two dozen regional offices had been established.

Along with the routine work of guarding against bank, store and hotel thieves, the Burns Agency was asked that first winter to investigate the Western Indiana Railroad's suspicion that it was being robbed by its own officials, which it was. A similar appeal soon came from the larger Illinois Central, where Burns turned up evidence that several department heads and one vice president were involved in a kickback scheme with railroad car repair companies. This case focused national attention on Burns as a private detective when Lincoln Steffens wrote about it in an *American Magazine* article. Then Burns was summoned by the Chicago & Western Railroad, where he discovered that executives had been buying up a needed right-of-way and then reselling it to themselves at a windfall profit.

His new agency was riding this string of successes when two mysterious explosions sounded almost simultaneously in Peoria, Illinois, on the night of September 4, 1910. The steel firm of McClintock, Marshall & Co. asked Burns to investigate. He hesitated for some time before agreeing to accept the case. He knew that a bitter dispute had been raging for years between a number of steel companies and the labor unions that had partially organized their employees, chiefly over the question of a closed or open shop. Acts of destruction against steel-company property had become increasingly frequent, with company spokesmen angrily accusing the unions, and unionists denying any knowledge of the incidents, passing them off as industrial accidents or staged attempts by the steel firms themselves to discredit unionism. The last thing Burns wanted was to risk having his new detective agency inherit the reputation of its competitors by involving himself and his men in anything resembling a labor dispute.

Still, he also reasoned that conducting a criminal investigation of alleged sabotage could hardly be called strikebreaking. And leaders of organized labor claimed to be as anxious as the steel companies to see the mysterious wave of incidents solved. As the man who had investigated Union-Labor Party men and corporation officials alike in San Francisco, and who had recently secured the evidence that brought high executives of three railroads into court, Burns had a right to believe his reputation for impartiality would remain secure. Although McClintock, Marshall & Co. admittedly suspected unionists, the firm agreed that the Burns Agency was being retained solely to hunt down the sabateurs, whoever they might be. Satisfied on this point, Burns dispatched a squad of his operatives to Peoria.

One explosion had wrecked girders in a railroad yard, the Burns men learned, while the other destroyed a crane in a foundry. And the agents soon discovered that a third explosion had been planned. Still intact in another stack of girders was a device consisting of an alarm clock and a small battery mounted on a board about nine inches long, connected with wires to a fulminate of mercury cap in a 10-quart can of nitroglycerin.

This bomb was as simple as it was deadly. Anyone using it could set the alarm for a given hour and be miles away when it went off, with the winding key turning to close a soldered contact and complete the circuit. Even when one of the tricky caps failed to explode, as in this case, the device was almost impossible to trace, since all of the parts were common hardware stock.

Still, there was a mill label on the nitroglycerin can that could be traced. The can turned out to have once been the property of the Independent Torpedo Company of Portland, Indiana, about 200 miles away. A check of recent customers there ended with suspicion centering on a man who called himself "J. W. McGraw." The Portland people recalled that McGraw was short, round-faced and wore a cap. He had said that he was buying the explosive for a quarry in Indianapolis. Investigation revealed that the quarry didn't exist. Probing further, the Burns agents found some sawdust in a livery-stable wagon McGraw had rented which matched sawdust found with the unexploded bomb. A sample of his handwriting was obtained from a hotel register, along with further descriptions of the man.

This was the progress made on the case by late September when William J. Burns left his son Raymond in charge and caught a train for Los Angeles where he was scheduled to attend the annual convention of his largest client, the American Bankers Association. It was while he was sleeping on that train that the blast occurred in his destination city which proved far more serious then the destruction of any number

164

of girders. Of the one hundred employees who had been trapped in the Los Angeles *Times'* building, few escaped without serious injury, and twenty-one were dead.

A porter awakened Burns with the news, handing him an urgent wire from Los Angeles Mayor George B. Alexander. The detective shook the sleep from his head and began sending telegrams himself: an acceptance to Alexander, a request to Raymond to have certain operatives join him, announcements of this new major assignment to all four of his West Coast offices, and a wire asking his Los Angeles district manager, Malcolm McLaren, to substitute for him at the bankers' convention.

A municipal detective met Burns at the station, and they drove directly to the wreckage that had once been a newspaper plant. Little could be learned from the still-smoking debris, but a strange suitcase was found late that morning in the home of *Times'* owner Harrison Gray Otis. Police carried it a safe distance from the house, started slitting it open, and suddenly heard a whirring sound. Only by diving into a ditch did they survive a blast that left a deep crater in the ground. Then another suitcase was discovered at the home of the secretary of the local Merchants and Manufacturers Association. This time the police managed to cut the wires and save the device.

It was when Burns examined this still-intact bomb that he suspected he had already been working on the case for fully four weeks. The contents of the suitcase were identical in every detail to the unexploded bomb in Peoria, except for the use of 16 sticks of "80%" dynamite instead of nitroglycerin.

When Burns met with Mayor Alexander that afternoon, the mayor made no secret of the fact that he was hiring reputation as well as skill. Already, the bitterly antilabor publisher Otis had managed to bring out a single-sheet extra on borrowed presses with a headline charging, UNIONIST BOMB WRECKS THE "TIMES." Alexander had no doubt that

Otis and others would do all in their power to use the tragedy to start a labor-baiting witch hunt.

Union officials all over the country were hotly denying the accusations. A typical statement had been made to newsmen in Indianapolis by Secretary-Treasurer John J. McNamara of the International Association of Bridge and Structural Ironworkers, the very union most frequently accused by the steel companies of sabotage. "Such an act is anarchy, pure and simple," he had asserted. "No sane individual or organization would resort to anything of the kind under any circumstances."

Mayor Alexander hoped that the retention of an outside investigator, a detective famed for prosecuting representatives of labor and capital alike, would reassure the unions, thwart the vengeance of their enemies, and encourage the general public to withhold judgment. "It looks like we've got a madman running around with enough dynamite to blow up all Los Angeles," the mayor, clearly frightened, told Burns. "We don't need a labor war as well."

Burns agreed, and following the pattern of the Peoria case, he set out to learn who had recently purchased eighty percent dynamite and where. Since dynamite so powerful was rarely used and was usually custom-produced when needed, he expected quick results from his West Coast men, and he got them. A call soon came from his San Francisco district office. The Du Pont Company there had filled an order for this grade of explosive little more than a week earlier.

The customer, a beefy, red-faced man who signed himself "Leonard," had claimed he needed the dynamite for uprooting tree stumps. Told that the requested grade was far too powerful and dangerous for this purpose, and was used only for quarry work in the hardest rock, Leonard had said: "Well, we got some boulders to be blasted too. Anyway," he added, "the boss wants eighty percent and I have to get it." The boss had turned out to be a thin, unkempt man who identified himself as "J. B. Bryce" when he, Leonard and a dark-haired little fellow who signed the delivery slip "Morris" came to pick up their purchase. They carefully loaded it into a small powerboat which bore the name *Pastime*.

Burns personally checked the descriptions of this trio by questioning all powder-company employees who had dealt with them. And he was left puzzled. By no stretch of the imagination could any of them be the J. W. McGraw of the Peoria case. Yet the two detonating mechanisms had been much too similar to be a coincidence.

The obvious next step was a thorough check of all boat rentals. At first, this turned into another puzzle. There simply was no record of any power craft called the *Pastime*. There was, however, one man on the docks who mentioned that some recent customers had rented his boat, the *Peerless*, and returned it with bow and stern freshly painted, its name newly and neatly lettered. A few minutes of paint scraping confirmed a suspicion that the *Peerless* had been the *Pastime* throughout at least one crucial cruise.

The address that the boat-rental man had been given turned out to be a vacant lot in south San Francisco. But this very fact suggested to Burns that the men he was hunting knew the neighborhood. He concentrated his own men on a systematic search that ended in an upstairs back room of a deserted house. There, under a new canvas tarpaulin, lay a cache of eighty percent dynamite — an amount just 48 sticks or three bombs short of the purchase made from the Du Pont Company.

A check of merchants who sold canvas came next, turning up a hardware store owner who remembered a little man answering the description of the alleged Morris, though he called himself "Capp." Nearby roominghouses were queried, and a landlady recalled a dark-haired "sneaky-looking" fellow named "William Capp" who had frequently been visited by a large, ruddy-faced man resembling the so-called Leonard. A search for sound-alike names in the city directory settled,

after endless elimination, on a recent resident named David
Caplan with a big, red-complexioned friend whose real name
was Matthew A. Schmidt.

About two weeks had gone by since the bombing, and
the trend of the trackdown seemed clear. Both Caplan and
Schmidt were notorious anarchists, of a fringe cult of the era
that had no known connection with organized labor or anything else that was organized. The anarchists were a loosely-
federated group opposed to government, marriage and social
restraints in general. Over the years, more than a few followers of the faith had expressed that opposition with bombs.
Neither Caplan nor Schmidt was a member of any union.
Although the real identity of their leader, J. B. Bryce, remained a mystery, it was logical to suspect that he was
another fanatic extremist.

From all signs so far, the hands of labor were clean.

But back in Los Angeles, furious with the mayor for
retaining the Burns Agency and for refusing to accept without
question the idea that unions were responsible for the bombing, Harrison Gray Otis was carrying his tirades against
unionism to such extremes that he actually seemed to be
welcoming the destruction of his newspaper for the opportunity
it gave him. What Otis and other antilabor men wanted and
were powerful enough to get was an open public hearing
where all their accusations could be aired. Three weeks after
the explosion, a special grand jury was convened and a
special prosecutor was appointed — a man Otis had praised as
fervently as he had condemned Burns: attorney Earl Rogers.

Burns had no time to worry about the encounters with
Rogers that would lie ahead. J. B. Bryce was still a mystery
and it soon became apparent that all three men had left the
state. Now Burns began the hard, slow task of back tracking
the trio, of tracing their movements prior to the bombing of
the *Times* building.

Dozens of false leads had to be run down for every one
that checked out, but the sketchy trail took him steadily north-
ward. His Portland office reported that the three men had

passed through that city in mid-September. Seattle seemed to be where the three had joined forces, and the Burns office there had located an electrician named J. D. Waggoner who recalled someone resembling J. B. Bryce asking questions about the possibility of detonating dynamite by direct electrical spark, rather than using the unreliable fulminating caps. Caplan and Schmidt could be backtracked to a squalid shacktown called the Home Colony, a known anarchist hangout, but they hadn't been seen there since early September, and their mysterious companion hadn't been with them then.

Just as the trail was fading out in the state of Washington, it turned hot and fresh in the Midwest. Over crosscountry wires came a call as compelling as the baying of a hound striking strong new scent. Burns caught the next train eastward. His son Raymond had located and identified the J. W. McGraw of the Peoria case.

The operatives Raymond Burns commanded had checked out a good many short round-faced men who had been seen in Portland, Indiana, and Peoria. When they spotted such a fellow named Ortie McManigal in Indianapolis and followed him to Chicago, he had seemed the least likely of the lot at first. A man with a wife and six children, he was hardly an anarchist or a fanatic of any sort. He didn't even have any known association with a trade union.

What intrigued Raymond Burns, though, was the fact that McManigal didn't have any known association with any trade, either. None of the man's neighbors had the slightest notion of what he did for a living, except that he was away for long periods of time and never seemed to lack for money. Samples of his handwriting were quietly obtained and compared with the signature on the hotel register. Salesmen from the Independent Torpedo Company were brought up for an unobtrusive glimpse of him. Witnesses and handwriting experts alike nodded emphatically. Ortie McManigal was the man who had purchased and transported the nitroglycerin found at Peoria.

As a result, when William J. Burns stepped down from a train at the Chicago station, his conviction that there was a link between the two bombing cases raised far more questions than it answered. What connection could there be between McManigal — a hired saboteur, from all appearances — and a pair of crazed radicals like Caplan and Schmidt?

"Those two bombs were made by the same man," Burns stubbornly asserted, but there was little the Burns Agency could do for the moment but keep watch on McManigal and intensify the search for the two known anarchists and the unknown J. B. Bryce.

Meanwhile other fireworks were exploding noisily in Los Angeles. The grand jury had convened and Earl Rogers never missed an opportunity to remind his audience that the city-financed Burns investigation had as yet produced no tangible results. This hardly surprised Burns, but the next move Rogers made left him shaking his head. After questioning a total of 174 witnesses to determine what the local police had insisted from the beginning — that the blast had been a dynamiting and not an accidental explosion — the elegant Rogers stayed in the center of the stage by publicly turning detective himself. With his old friend Luther Brown and some investigators borrowed from the district attorney's staff, Earl Rogers began looking for purchasers of eighty percent dynamite.

Then the case came alive again in Chicago. Little Ortie McManigal set out for the railroad station one day, carrying an encased rifle and some camping equipment. He caught a train for Kenosha, Wisconsin, apparently bound for nothing more sinister than a week of deer hunting in the northwoods. At Kenosha, he picked up a hunting companion who signed himself "Frank Sullivan" on the hotel registers. It was Sullivan's description, though — "thin, narrow shoulders, pinched cheeks, sunken eyes, stringy hair" — that caused Burns to send two of his best men on a deer-hunting trip of their own.

There was nothing unusual, in as good a stretch of cover as the brush between Eagle River and Three Lakes offered, for two hunting camps to be set up within a few hundred yards of each other. Nor was there anything to arouse suspicion when the two pairs of hunters met in the woods, fell into the easy sociability of outdoorsmen, and ended up camping together. Neither Ortie McManigal nor his companion from Kenosha thought to object when one of their new-found friends wanted to take a snapshot by way of remembering their good times together.

When William J. Burns went westward again, he carried an enlarged portion of that snapshot. He showed the photo to witnesses everywhere from Seattle to San Francisco, and sent a copy to the Los Angeles County district attorney's office as well. From all sources, he received the reply he'd expected. The *Times* building bombing and the Peoria explosions were finally connected by more than a mere similarity of detonating devices. The alleged Frank Sullivan and the elusive J. B. Bryce were one and the same.

Just who the man really was remained to be seen. As Burns started back for Chicago to begin finding out, a long-brewing storm broke behine him. Earl Rogers had steadily insisted to the Los Angeles grand jury and to the press that the city was being swindled by his old enemy from the graft prosecutions. Burns' blithe flashing of a photo of the leader of the dynamite-purchasing trio — disheartening proof to Rogers that the detective was far ahead of him on the trail — bared the worst of the bitter grudge the attorney had been nursing for years. Where had the picture been taken? he demanded to know. Who was the man?

When no answers were forthcoming, Rogers angrily called Mayor George Alexander before the grand jury. What were the taxpayers getting for their money? he demanded. What *evidence* was the Burns investigation producing? The mayor didn't know, and the grand jury learned little more by questioning the Burns district manager. Then the Burns office was broken into one night and thoroughly ransacked.

Fortunately, all information that might have jeopardized

the manhunt was safe in Chicago. But under mounting pressure, Mayor Alexander was forced to ask for daily reports from the agency in the future. At that critical moment of the chase, when secrecy was so important that Burns operatives had orders to lose the suspects they were shadowing rather than risk betraying themselves, the request had to be refused. The City of Los Angeles cut off all further funds from the Burns Agency.

"The end of it," William J. Burns later reported, "was that I had to go ahead and finance the investigation myself. It cost me $14,000."

To be sure, rewards had been offered for the capture of the dynamiters. But rewards were notoriously unreliable, frequently withdrawn and almost invariably disputed. They were hardly a source of income upon which a national detective agency could depend. The firm of McClintock, Marshall & Co. could be fairly billed only for the Peoria investigation and the surveillance of McManigal, not for a countrywide operation. Fourteen thousand dollars was a sizable sum of money in 1910, particularly to a man who lived most of his life on a Secret Service salary. But Burns had no thought of abandoning the hunt.

"I knew that our operatives were watching the right rat holes," he added, "and I intended to keep them there as long as I could raise the money to pay their wages."

At the moment, the chief rat holes to be watched were the saloons of Chicago, where Ortie McManigal and his mysterious friend spent more than a month carousing together after they returned from Wisconsin. Then they suddenly set out for Ohio, where they visited an older man, who proved to be McManigal's father, on a farm near Tiffin. The pair split up upon leaving. The gaunt mystery man now was trailed to Cincinnati, where he turned out to be rejoining his widowed mother, a Mrs. McNamara.

The fact that J. B. Bryce, alias Frank Sullivan, could at last be identified as one James B. McNamara — a reform school graduate, unmarried, of poor reputation — meant little in itself. The fact that James had a fleshier, well-known older brother named John meant much more, particularly when Ortie McManigal was followed directly to John Mc-Namara's office.

McClintock, Marshall & Co. had been right all along. So had stiff-necked old Harrison Gray Otis. Because John J. McNamara was the very union official who had issued the press release after the Los Angeles explosion, stating, "Such an act is anarchy, pure and simple."

Burns felt that he had more than enough evidence to convict McManigal and James McNamara, but he knew that to arrest either now would almost certainly destroy any chance he had of getting John McNamara. No one was likely to catch the Secretary-Treasurer of the International Association of Bridge and Structural Iron workers — respected in the highest circles of organized labor and a close friend of American Federation of Labor President Samuel Gompers — carrying dynamite around in a handbag. A conclusive link had to be established between John McNamara, the known bombers, and the bombings themselves, and Burns realized that it might take a long time to do it.

The big danger lay in what McManigal and Jim Mc-Namara might do if they remained free men. At Christmas time, Burns found out. Slipping out of Chicago, Ortie Mc-Manigal celebrated the holiday season by journeying to Los Angeles and blowing up the Llewellyn Iron Works. Luckily, no lives were lost. Burns wrestled with his conscience and decided he had to gamble once more. Warning his operatives that to let either man out of their sight could prove disastrous, and redoubling the efforts of the agents checking into the affairs of the union official in Indianapolis, Burns waited for the break in the case he felt sure had to come.

Early in April, Burns made a quick trip to Boston to see a client. While he was there, both McManigal and the younger McNamara brother left their respective homes in

173

Chicago and Cincinnati and boarded trains almost simultaneously. Their trails merged in Toledo, and on April 11, a terse telegram went off to the Burns headquarters in Chicago: NUMBER ONE MET NUMBER TWO. Raymond Burns wired his father the news, then quietly brought the Chicago police into the case, borrowing a pair of municipal detectives and setting out at once.

Joining his men in Toledo at a hotel across the street from the one in which the suspects were staying, Raymond Burns posted a tight watch and maintained it through the night. The next morning it became obvious that the dynamiters intended doing no work in the town where they had met. Instead, they caught a train for Detroit, keeping their heavy suitcases beside them in the crowded day coach. Positive that the suitcases carried explosives, Raymond Burns and the Chicago officers winced with each jolt of the train ride.

As the train slowly rumbled through the outskirts of Detroit, McManigal and McNamara showed a great deal of interest in several bridges they saw. When the train at last reached the station, the two men refused the help of porters. Lugging their own bags, they went out to begin wandering warily about the streets in a patternless manner, obviously checking for followers. Apparently satisfied, they entered the Oxford Hotel.

The lobby was even more crowded than the day coach had been. A theatrical company had just arrived and was checking in. As heatedly as McNamara argued with the desk clerk, he couldn't get a room immediately, and at last accepted the promise of a room later on in the day. When the clerk suggested that the two men check their bags, McNamara hesitated. Then he shrugged, handed over his suitcase, and started impatiently for the door. McManigal, clearly exhausted was only too happy to do the same.

This was the moment Raymond Burns had been looking for. Twisting and dodging through the crowd, he caught McManigal still at the desk, jammed a revolver against him, and

174

threw on a pair of handcuffs. Before McNamara could whip around, he was pinned, too.

While McNamara raged, the two Chicago detectives identified themselves, demanded the luggage from the clerk and found not only the makings of bombs inside but also a pair of revolvers and a rifle with a Maxim silencer.

To explain the presence of Chicago's police in Detroit, Raymond informed McNamara and McManigal that they were wanted for blowing a safe in Chicago the previous Saturday night. It was a clever plan, and it worked. McNamara had been with his mother in Cincinnati that evening, as the Burns men knew well, and McManigal had been shopping with his family on State Street. Confident of their alibis and anxious to get out of Detroit where the discovery of their arsenal could mean serious trouble, both men signed extradition papers at the police station.

Even so, James McNamara grew suspicious on the train trip westward. "You don't want me for a Chicago job," he said accusingly. "You want me for a Los Angeles job."

Raymond Burns remained silent.

Finally McNamara blurted, "You can have $20,000 if you let me get away."

"That's not enough," Raymond told him, straight-faced. "It would have to go too many ways."

"Thirty thousand then."

"Where would you get that kind of money?"

"From the . . . Don't you worry about that. Just give me ten minutes in any telegraph office."

Raymond Burns tried again. "Who thinks you're worth $30,000?"

McNamara lapsed into a long sullen silence. Then he started talking, neither admitting nor denying anything, but justifying whatever had to be done to advance the cause of organized labor.

"How does it help organized labor to kill a bunch of working people?" Raymond couldn't help wondering.

175

"I'd blow up the whole goddamned country if it'd get us our rights." McNamara half-screamed, seemingly on the edge of hysteria. Then, keeping his nervous fingers busy by rolling and chain-smoking cigarettes, he turned silent again.

William J. Burns was waiting at the Chicago station. With local authorities cooperating fully, the two men were formally charged with bombing the Los Angeles *Times* and first-degree murder. Jim McNamara seemed resigned to this by then, but McManigal was shocked and horrified. He wanted to see Burns alone.

"I didn't have anything to do with the *Times* building job," he protested. "Jim did that one with the help of a couple of anarchists named Schmidt and Caplan. I wasn't even there."

"We know that," Burns nodded. "But it doesn't really matter." He went on to explain the laws of conspiracy, and what being an accessory after the fact meant.

McManigal looked as if he could already feel a thick hemp rope around his neck. "If I told everything I knew, would things go easy on me?" he asked.

"I can't promise you a thing," Burns told him. "I'm only a private detective, and I don't have the authority. Any decision about reducing the charges would have to be made by the Los Angeles district attorney's office, and sentencing would be up to the presiding judge in the case. All that I or anyone else in Chicago can do is report your cooperation or the lack of it."

That was enough for Ortie McManigal. He started talking and talking fast. He told of planting the three bombs in Peoria, and dynamiting the Llewellyn Iron Works on the coast, the Iroquois Iron Company in Chicago, and a long list of other establishments. He explained how he and Jim McNamara usually sent newspaper clippings to John McNamara as proof they had carried out an assignment, and received $200 apiece for each; the money was listed under "Organizing Work" on the books of the Ironworkers union.

No payments went to men like Caplan and Schmidt, Mc-
Manigal said, because the union official could take advantage of their weird philosophy to get his dynamiting done
for nothing. McManigal gave the locations of various caches
of explosives and bomb parts. He talked for hours in a rapid,
high-pitched voice, repeating himself four and five times,
incessantly insisting that he didn't want to hang.

William J. Burns had already wired Los Angeles request-
ing extradition papers, but he knew he still had a long wait
before a third arrest could be made. The Chicago authorities
had promised to keep the arrests of McManigal and Jim
McNamara quiet, but some way had to be found to prevent
John J. McNamara from getting suspicious when he heard
nothing about any explosions in Detroit. Given even a few
hours' warning, the man could destroy enough evidence to
save himself. The plan Burns decided upon was simplicity
itself. He merely picked up a phone and called Mrs. Mc-
Manigal.

"You don't know me, and I don't know you," he
muttered in a rough voice, "but I got a letter this morning
with your number in it. The letter says, 'Call this number
immediately, and tell the woman there her husband is all
right. He and his friend were arrested for safe-blowing, but
it was a mistake. The police let them go, and they're in
Windsor.' "

"Good," the lady gasped. "Lord, that's good news to
me."

"Just listen." Burns ordered her, pretending to read
on. " 'Tell her to go to a certain party . . . . ' There's
no name given, but . . . "

"I know," Mrs. McManigal assured him. "I know."

"Tell her to go to a certain party and get $500 from
him, then go back home and wait until she hears from her
husband.' That's all it says."

That was all that was needed. McManigal's wife was

followed as she caught the next train for Indianapolis. And after her visit the Burns men who were watching John McNamara reported no sign of panic or suspicion.

It was April 21 before a representative of the Los Angeles district attorney's office arrived — not Special Prosecutor Earl Rogers, Burns noted with relief, but Assistant District Attorney Joseph Ford, who brought several of his own men and the necessary papers. Extradition documents were signed not only by the governor of Illinois, but a paper was signed the next morning by the governor of Indiana as well. Then, with Burns men deliberately remaining in the background, the Indianapolis police broke into a meeting of the executive board of the Ironworkers' union and took the secretary-treasurer into custody. John McNamara was a tall man like his brother, but heavier, and he had a weird permanent smile on his full face. Within a few hours, he had been brought before a local judge, who examined the extradition papers, found them in order, and handed McNamara over to the Los Angeles detectives.

Those few hours were the busiest the William J. Burns National Detective Agency had ever known. Armed with warrants that had been readied in advance, its operatives carried out a rapid series of raids, each accompanied by an Indianapolis policeman. The union's books were seized, and Burns nodded in satisfaction when he saw that the "Organizing Work" account McManigal had mentioned was a completely separate item from the salaries and expenses of the legitimate organizers.

In a basement vault of the same office building, Burns found dynamite and caps, other electrical items and fourteen small alarm clocks. Similar equipment was discovered in the bedroom of John McNamara's apartment. Numerous other leads were checked out, with the mounting evidence becoming ever more conclusive. On a nearby farm, where the secretary-treasurer had rented space for storing supposed "union records," a large piano box was located containing both dynamite and nitroglycerin packed in sawdust. Just four hours after effecting the arrest of an influential man on little more than faith in the story of a confederate, Burns had an ironclad case.

"I don't think even a bribed jury would dare acquit them now," he told Assistant D. A. Ford, with all three prisoners already on their way to California under guard.

Burns had no way of knowing that this chance allusion to bribery would prove to be far more than a figure of speech. Nor could he know, at that moment, some six months after he'd set out on the chase, what a figure of controversy he would become before the next six months went by. His only concern had been to catch the guilty men. The fact that James McNamara was listed on the rolls as a member and John was a high official of one of the most powerful unions in the American Federation of Labor could not erase the fact that they were also unmistakably the mass-murderers of twenty-one people.

Even if Burns had foreseen what was coming, he would have handled the case no differently. But his step might have been less light, and his grin not quite so genial as he returned to his hotel and greeted a growing crowd of reporters.

UNION LEADER ARRESTED FOR BOMB OUTRAGE . . . BURNS HAS THE CONFESSION OF A DYNAMITER read the headlines of *The New York Times* on April 23, 1911. Similar headlines blazed from every newsstand in North America, in London, and almost everywhere else in the world. After months of obscurity, William J. Burns was a front-page figure once more. ALL GOOD AMERICAN CITIZENS FEEL THAT THEY OWE YOU A DEBT OF GRATITUDE FOR YOUR SIGNAL SERVICE TO AMERICAN CITIZENSHIP, President Roosevelt wired. A whole nation agreed and wanted the details.

When Burns made a trip to his headquarters office in Chicago that day, his train was mobbed by newsmen. Arriving at the station, he was inundated by another swarm of report-

ers. And when he returned to Indianapolis to begin document-
ing and double-checking loose ends of the dynamiting case,
the Indiana capital seemed to be hosting a newspaperman's
convention.

Burns hardly seemed harassed. He gloried in being back
on center stage again. He was a newsman's delight, answering virtually every question tossed his way and even re-enact-
ing some of the high points of the investigation. Veteran
reporters from great dailies throughout the nation filed unabashedly worshipful stories, the same kind of tributes Lincoln
Steffens had written about Burns' work on the land-frauds,
graft, and railroad investigations.

When Burns finally left town again, a *McClure's Magazine* writer named Harvey J. O'Higgins slipped into a Pull-
man compartment with him. The resulting copy was typical
of the prose pouring forth at this moment of triumph:

> Here he was, then — the great detective who had
> proved himself cleverer than the cleverest counterfeiters
> that the country could produce, who had come out of
> the government Secret Service with the name of being
> the best operative that the department had ever known,
> who had made possible the success of the graft investi-
> gation in San Francisco and ferreted out evidence of the
> public-lands frauds in Oregon and California, and pitted
> himself against public corruptionists and railroad thieves
> and bribe-taking legislators and murderers and dynamiters
> successfully, without a failure, year after year . . . Here
> he was — one of the most conspicuous veterans of the
> social struggle of our day, apparently perfect for his
> particular work in the world . . . What was the power
> hidden in him that had made him what he was?
>
> He had been for three days in Indianapolis, cleaning
> up the evidence against the men whom he had arrested
> for dynamiting the Los Angeles *Times* building in Cali-
> fornia; and during those three days he had been living,
> like a celebrity on tour, in the eyes of all the report-
> ers . . . He had moved through this observation and sur-

The Great Dynamite Conspiracy

The Accused Labor Leaders, the Man Who Accuses Them and the Scene of the Outrages That Shocked a Continent

W. J. BURNS DETECTIVE (AT LEFT), J. J. McNAMARA, PRISONER (AT RIGHT), AND McNAMARA'S HOME IN CINCINNATI, O.

Burns is the detective who charges McNamara with plotting the dynamite explosions in Los Angeles and a dozen other cities. McNamara who protests his innocence, asserts he is the victim of a conspiracy to injure union labor. Conservative citizens withhold judgment until all the evidence is heard.

From a newspaper feature story about the McNamara case

William J. Burns (left front), Wilson (right front), Sheriff Teager of
Los Angeles (left rear), and Chief of Police Louis Oakes of Los Angeles

Crowd watching for the McNamaras, December 1911

veillance with an easy, jovial manner, laughing and talking in the hotel lobby or on the street, without a trace of the manner of the traditional sleuth, without so much as a glance behind him or a confidential word out of the corner of his mouth. And during the whole time he had been secretly meeting and directing his operatives, consulting with the police, and gathering by telephone and telegraph the evidence and corroboration of witnesses against the men whose movements for months past he had been carrying — mapped out to the last detail — in the silence that lay behind his breezy public manner and his candid, uncunning smile.

William J. Burns is concededly a great detective; but anyone who had watched him for those three days would hardly have suspected that he was a detective at all. His art is the sort that conceals itself naturally as if in the mysteries of intuition. Not only is his personal appearance a perfect disguise, but the outward habit of his mind is as good as an alias. His portraits represent him as a large, dark, presumably slow-moving person of the well-known police-captain type. Actually, he is red, brisk, rather small in stature, with the appearance of a prosperous businessman, quick in his movements and gestures, and altogether dynamic in his effect.

But then, very gradually, the tone of some of the press coverage started to change. Samuel Gompers, President of the American Federation of Labor throughout all but two years of its 25-year history, began angrily asserting that the arrest of the two brothers was merely a vicious attempt to discredit unionism, carried out "as usual, by a private detective agency," an inhuman scheme to destroy the Ironworkers at the cost of the lives of innocent men.

"Labor has no intention," he promised grimly, "of turning its back on John and Jim McNamara."

On learning of Gompers' attack, Burns did his best to clear the air. "If Mr. Gompers will just sit down with me, at his convenience," he said, "I am certain I can convince him this is strictly a criminal case and does not concern

organized labor. If need be, I will even show him evidence
that cannot be made public as yet."

Gompers' only response was to remind reporters that
private detectives had planted evidence and trumped up confessions in the past. He made a trip to Indianapolis while
Burns was still in the city, but he sat down only with the
Ironworkers' officials and listened only to their assurances
that the accused men were innocent. He soon had two decisive
announcements to make to the press.

The American Federation of Labor was launching a
nationwide campaign to raise a $300,000 defense fund for the
McNamara brothers. And heading the defense team, hired
for a $50,000 fee and $100-a-day expenses, would be the
nation's most famous labor lawyer, the man who had made
headlines when he successfully represented Eugene Debs of
the Railroad Brotherhoods and "Big Bill" Haywood of the
I.W.W., the attorney known as the "Great Defender," Clarence Darrow.

A tall slouch-shouldered man in his mid-50's with a
perpetually sad face beneath a great shock of uncombed hair,
Darrow went directly to Los Angeles to confer with his clients.
He then pleaded them not guilty. The McNamaras, he
announced in beginning a barrage of effectively worded press
statements, were "pawns in a vast industrial war," victims of
a "capitalistic conspiracy" that had been financed by "the
steel trust with its gold" and "masterminded by William J.
Burns."

The Great Defender's words carried weight. Workingmen
read them and went without lunches to contribute to the
McNamara defense fund. His ringing phrases were echoed
not only in the highest circles of organized labor but throughout the entire spectrum of left-wing society, at a time when
the Socialist Party was approaching the peak of its voting
strength in the United States. Before long, some of the very
newspapers that had been most emphatic in praising Burns'
feat of crime detection were beginning to backtrack and raise
doubts, to cushion their reputations for editorial wisdom
against the reaction that would come should Darrow's accusations prove true.

Burns tried hard to stem the trend. "I'm no respecter

of persons when they're criminals,'' he told one interviewing reporter, and earnestly went on to express his creed as a detective. "If I'd found evidence in this case to implicate the president of the largest corporation in the United States, and the board of directors, I'd have been right after them all. That's my business, my calling. I'm conducting a detective agency. When I'm employed to find out who committed a crime, I go out to find him. I don't care a row of red apples who he is or where he is. These people who are calling me an 'enemy of labor' for running down these dynamiters are as muddleheaded as the jawsmiths in San Francisco who called me an 'enemy of capital' for going after the big fellows in the graft investigation out there. When I have my case against a criminal, I put my clamps on him just as quick whether he has diamond rings on his fingers or callouses as big as hoofs.''

But there was no way he could keep the case from becoming a capital-labor controversy. With a battle cry of "Save the McNamaras!" the defense-fund drive was rapidly assuming the proportions of a crusade. Like circuit-riding evangelists, labor leaders were making whirlwind speaking tours, rousing a revivalistic fervor in union halls everywhere. Clarence Darrow's claim that the surprise arrest and rapid extradition of John McNamara were illegal was widely publicized. By June 16, an Indianapolis grand jury was actually indicting William J. Burns for kidnapping.

This was no more than a minor irritation for Burns, a matter of submitting to formal arrest with bond already posted. But the pro-McNamara campaign was gaining more ominous aspects. Notes and phone calls threatening Burns' life were coming in so frequently that he felt compelled to announce that even a successful attempt on his life would not prevent the conviction of the two brothers. He told the press that he had given a detailed summary of the case and duplicate copies of all documents to someone who would carry on for him if he were killed. He wasn't bluffing. That someone was Frank Heney, now living quietly in Pueblo, Colorado.

At every opportunity, District Attorney John D. Fredericks of Los Angeles County and his assistant Joe Ford insisted that there was no antilabor conspiracy, that Burns had given them an airtight criminal case. But prosecutors were expected to show such confidence, and Darrow simply charged that they, too, were part of a steel-trust plot.

Through those late-summer and early-autumn months of 1911, when the McNamara brothers were being proclaimed "Heroes of Labor" and the detective who had run them down was being subjected to thunderous abuse, one important voice that might have been raised in Burns' behalf was notably quiet. In completing his temporary role with the grand jury, attorney Earl Rogers had access to all the evidence Burns had amassed. Privately, he accepted the fact that the McNamaras were guilty. But the old hatred lingered. As the attacks on Burns mounted, Rogers watched in silence, and probably in satisfaction as well.

One by one, newspapers were modifying their estimates of the case and changing their tone. Some switched sides outright. Before long, even in the city where the mass murder had been committed, such newspapers as the Los Angeles *Record* were asserting in news columns as well as on the editorial page that the McNamaras were innocent. But the biggest blow for William J. Burns came when the great Lincoln Steffens, the journalist who had been praising him wholeheartedly for nearly a decade, lent a pen to the cause of the McNamaras.

The abrupt reversal of his press relations angered Burns, but there was important work to be done. The hunt for Caplan and Schmidt had to go on. Trips had to be made to the coast to confer with Fredericks and Ford. Witnesses had to be watched and guarded. Salesman C. C. Keiser of the Independent Torpedo Company, who had sold large quantities of nitroglycerin directly to John McNamara, needed the constant protection of Burns men once his identity was learned, as did electrician J. D. Waggoner of Seattle and Superintendent Phillips of the Du Pont Powder Works in San

Francisco. A hotel clerk named Diekelman, one of the witnesses who had identified Jim McNamara as J. B. Bryce, suddenly vanished from Los Angeles. An immediate alert to the entire Burns network located him in Albuquerque, New Mexico, being wined and dined by a man named Hammerstrohm, who happened to be Clarence Darrow's brother-in-law. On to Chicago this high-living pair went, only to find Raymond Burns waiting at the door of Darrow's law office.

"Do you want to back to L.A. on your own or on a D.A.'s warrant to wait in jail for the trial?" young Burns asked Diekelman. The hotel clerk went back on his own.

Once the selection of a McNamara jury began on October 17, there were veniremen to guard as well as witnesses. The very successful A.F.L. fund drive had not only furnished Clarence Darrow with assistant lawyers but with a platoon of investigators as well. Heading the investigators was a former deputy sheriff named Bert Franklin, who immediately began attempting to bribe jurors. He paid off one juror named Robert Bain, then tried another named George Lockwood. Lockwood told the police and assisted in setting a trap for Franklin. Fearful and conscience-stricken, Bain's wife provided added evidence by admitting her husband had taken the bribe. Soon, the chief defense investigator was under arrest himself.

But these were largely behind-the-scenes events, lost in the avalanche of accusations being hurled at Burns from the national bandwagon the McNamara campaign had become. Turning to what was still a novelty at the time, the fund raisers produced a movie portraying the plot against labor that Darrow was so eloquently describing. Two slightly built, boyishly handsome actors were hired to play the six-foot-tall McNamara brothers, while a huge wrestler type took the part of the relatively small Burns. The only touches of realism were officials of the Ironworkers Union who insisted upon playing themselves.

The film opened with Mrs. McNamara blessing her sons

as they went out into the world, then switched to some ferocious-looking capitalists in striped pants conspiring with their gigantic hireling Burns, who promptly kidnapped the boys, beating them savagely in the process. At the end, the McNamaras lifted their hands in prayer behind bars, after writing a "Letter to Labor" that was a wordier version of what a real frame-up victim named Joe Hill would say in a Utah prison five years later: "Don't mourn for me, boys — organize!"

As crude as the propaganda message was, it proved highly successful. The movie brought a fresh flood of donations when shown in union halls, and at the big McNamara rallies that were being staged complete with torchlight parades. Meantime, there were other sources of income. Socialists were holding McNamara balls in imitation of charity fund-raising affairs. Stamps with flattering pictures of the brothers were being sold like present-day Christmas seals for use on official union correspondence. Big red, white, and blue buttons with the same pictures were proclaiming THE McNAMARAS ARE INNOCENT on shirts and blouses alike, and similarly colored and worded banners were decorating buildings and homes in every major American city. McNamara sentiment ran so high in Los Angeles that sobbing women were massing outside the prisoners' cells and throwing kisses, and a Socialist candidate for mayor actually seemed to have a good chance of replacing George Alexander in the coming election after plastering the city with huge signs saying: SAVE THE McNAMARAS FROM THE CAPITALIST CONSPIRACY. ELECT JOB HARRIMAN.

But on December 1, 1911, there came what was probably the most momentous rug-pulling act in American history. The banners were torn down and furtively burned, the stamps decorated no more envelopes, the big buttons vanished, the movies shelved, and no more kisses were thrown at the county jail. Scheduled rallies and balls were hurriedly canceled, the editor of the Los Angeles *Record* fainted at his desk, and with all hope of becoming mayor gone forever, Job Harriman, like Samuel Gompers and a good many others, was left trying to convince the public that he was nothing worse than a fool. Because on that day, Jim and John McNamara changed their pleas, confessed, and threw themselves on the mercy of the court.

"It was the remarkable work of William J. Burns," Assistant District Attorney Joe Ford told amazed reporters, "that drove the defendants to confessions as a means of escaping the extreme penalty."

For the first time, the prosecution and defense were in agreement. "The McNamara brothers," one of Clarence Darrow's assistants explained, "were advised to plead guilty as the only course that could be followed to save their lives. The case against them worked up by Detective Burns was impregnable."

When newsman mobbed the detective at his headquarters office in Chicago, he seemed the least surprised man in America.

"I said last April that we had an ironclad case," he reminded them, "and we've been strengthening it ever since."

"What will you do with the reward money?" reporters asked. Estimates of the total of the various rewards offered had once ranged as high as $200,000, but many had been quietly withdrawn.

"Once the expenses still outstanding are covered," Burns promised, "it will be divided equally into bonuses for all operatives who worked on the case. But don't forget the job isn't finished. Caplan and Schmidt are still at large. And we're going to get them."

On December 5, 1911, James B. McNamara was sentenced to life imprisonment. His brother John, in the absence of proof that the *Times* building bombing was specifically ordered, was charged only with the Llewellyn Iron Works dynamiting and given fifteen years. Both went to San Quentin cells in the same block as the one occupied by San Francisco grafter Abraham Ruef.

Yet even then, the story stayed on the front pages. "My credulity was imposed upon," Samuel Gompers stated in embarrassment. "I raised $300,000 for their defense, believing them innocent." Lesser labor leaders declared that the fiasco had set their cause back fifty years. In one local union after another, rank-and-file members were passing resolutions praising Burns, condemning their own officials and frequently demanding the death penalty for the McNamaras as well. Through the entire 15-month-long drama of the dynamiting, only one major figure had emerged both clean-handed and consistent. A *New York Times* editorial expressed the national mood:

> Among the minor but highly satisfactory and far from unimportant consequences of the McNamara confessions is the brilliant vindication they give to William J. Burns, the greatest detective certainly, and perhaps the only really great detective, the only detective of genius, whom this country has produced. And the vindication is no less as to character than as to achievement. Of course we have in this profession other men of honesty as well as ability, of courage as well as intelligence. But in Mr. Burns there seems to be a unique combination of all the qualities that social servants of this class ought to possess . . . .
>
> And yet it is this man, with his long record of success in the hunting down of criminals — a record which is unblemished by a single suspicion of corruption that has any foundation of fact or evidence — who for months was violently assailed as conspirator who, for hire, had manufactured an elaborate case against innocent men . . . .
>
> For the belief that many, possibly a majority, of private detectives are crooked, we have the authority of Mr. Burns himself, but every unprejudiced student of

the times knows that he is "straight." He has proved it again and again, and never better than now.

This tribute was entitled "Apologies Due a Detective." But no such apologies came from the men who owed them most. Caught between the twin fires of rebellion in the ranks and the threat of a federal investigation, Gompers and his top lieutenants found no time to offer any public regrets for their six months of slander. And attorney Earl Rogers, who had aided that slander by his silence, began sniping away at his old enemy again almost immediately, suggesting it would be improper for Burns to receive the $25,000 reward Los Angeles had offered. Arguing that Burns had originally been retained by the city and that municipal employees were ineligible for such rewards, Rogers urged that the money go instead to investigator Sam Browne of the county district attorney's office, who had assisted Rogers when the lawyer had turned detective and retraced some early local phases of the Burns investigation.

Browne was surprised by the suggestion, though he quickly made it plain that giving this reward to him now sounded like a reasonable idea. But his own superior, the assistant district attorney, was indignant. "No one else tried to claim credit for capturing the McNamaras all those months half the country believed they were innocent," Joe Ford declared. "All the rewards should go to Burns."

Most significant of all, no apologies came from the man who had done most of the violent assailing, the man who had coined the ringing phrases about "a capitalistic conspiracy masterminded by William J. Burns." Clarence Darrow was, in fact, still singing that same song — but in his own defense now. For back when a trap had been set for jury-briber Bert Williams, far bigger game had walked in. To the amazement of police and Burns operatives alike, the Great Defender himself had appeared on the scene.

Darrow's story was that he had come in response to an

189

anonymous phone call, and that he had known nothing about the money being passed on the street. But he hadn't been too convincing. Jurors Lockwood and Bain both stated that they had been told from the beginning that Darrow was directing the payoffs. Williams, who pleaded guilty and was given a heavy fine, eventually implicated his former employer. On January 29, 1912, Clarence Darrow was indicted for attempting to bribe George Lockwood.

Burns was hardly surprised to hear Darrow warming over the old charges of a capitalist plot and sounding them again in his own behalf. But the next development in the case surprised Burns and a good many other people. For retained as Darrow's chief counsel, and soon echoing those same accusations of a conspiracy against unionism, was the very man who had headed the retinue of the trolley magnates in San Francisco where Patrick Calhoun had so ruthlessly smashed the carmen's union, the man who had served as special prosecutor for a grand jury investigation of the dynamiting and was currently disputing Burns' right to the McNamara reward — the able but alcoholic, brilliant but erratic Earl Rogers.

Exactly why Rogers took the Darrow case, he alone knew. Beyond doubt he needed the money, but he had refused lucrative cases before. He had involved philosophical explanations to offer his shocked friends and associates. But all of his polished mannerisms couldn't cover the near-psychotic grudge he had been nursing, and he may well have offered a better explanation one day when he muttered: "I've waited a long time for Mr. Burns to walk into my parlor."

Defending Darrow was certain to give him a chance to get William J. Burns on a witness stand.

Even before the detective arrived to testify, he had emerged as the key figure at that trial, which lasted twelve weeks. Rogers failed to shake the stories of juror Lockwood and briber Williams, and was forced to fall back on accusations that both witnesses were part of a conspiracy against Darrow masterminded by Burns. Finally Burns was sworn in to testify. A young reporter named Hugh Bailie, who was destined to become the president of the United Press, watched the long-awaited confrontation and wrote that Burns was one witness who "was taking no bullying from Rogers."

The elegant attorney had a favorite tactic designed to intimidate witnesses. He carried a long-handled pair of eye glasses and from time to time, especially during heated questioning, he would swing the glasses menacingly at the man on the stand. When he waved the lorgnette at Burns, the detective matched dramatics with dramatics. Throwing up his hands in mock horror, Burns begged the court to protect him from such a dangerous instrument. Rogers counter-ed by asking how he could endanger a man who carried a gun in his pocket and whose cane was really the case for a con-cealed sword. The detective could laugh at this, but the cross-examination became an unending series of shouts and in-sinuations. Day after day, this clash went on, and remarkably little of it had any bearing on the bribery charges against Clarence Darrow.

Outside of court, as Bailie observed, Burns regarded Rogers as "a well-bred hoodlum." Answering the questions of the newsmen who invariably clustered about him in the corridor, the detective would occasionally look over at the defense attorney and shake his head in disgust. On one occasion, the two men carried their duel out into that corri-dor and there was nothing well-bred about it. Stalking up to Burns, Rogers demanded: "Did you call me a son of a bitch, Mr. Burns?" and then took a wild, roundhouse swing at the detective. Burns, who hadn't said a word to Rogers, except from the witness stand, ducked and followed with a shove that sent the tall attorney sprawling.

Rogers eventually returned to the case being tried in his cross-examination, spouting a stream of rapid-fire questions designed to imply that Burns had bribed Williams to bribe Lockwood to get Darrow. Sensing that this tack was as hard

191

for the jury to follow as to believe, the lawyer suddenly switched his attack.

"There is a reward in the McNamara case, I believe?" There were several.

"You intend to claim this money?"

"I do."

"You think that you and you alone caught the McNamaras, with no help from Sam Browne and my humble self?"

"Rogers, you've been getting off a lot of bunk. I've heard something of your claim. It's a lot of rot. And it hasn't meant a thing to anyone, except maybe this fellow Browne."

Objections from the prosecution ended this line of questioning. But it was more than obvious that the defendant himself would have objected if courtroom procedure had permitted. Darrow was far from happy to hear the McNamara reward dragged into his case. Nor was he satisfied with much of anything else Earl Rogers had done, including the attorney's mysterious absences for days at a time, with the press and the public whispering that he was off on another drinking spree. Darrow later made it clear, in fact, that he believed he'd been given no defense.

When Darrow looked at the jury as the trial neared its conclusion, and he had looked at a great many in his day, he saw himself convicted. On August 14, 1912, he made his own final plea, a powerful, moving address that is still being cited for law students as a classic example of eloquence triumphing over evidence, ranking with the "Cross of Gold" speech of William Jennings Bryan, whom Darrow would face in a Tennessee courtroom on a much later day.

"Burns!" The rumpled lawyer with the stance that suggested the entire world's weight was on his shoulders spat out the name venomously. "Burns with his pack of hounds. The steel trust with its gold. All arrayed against me. I stood alone for the poor and weak.

"Will it be the gray dim walls of San Quentin?" Darrow

wondered plaintively. "My life has been all too human, but I have been a friend to the helpless. I have cried their cause."

Hour after hour, for fully a day and a half, he went on in this vein — sobs shaking his slouching body, his beautifully worded phrases contrasting sharply with his shaggy appearance. Then, choosing his climactic moment with a superb sense of timing, he staged his crucifixion scene.

"Oh, you wild insane members of the steel trust . . ." He rose on his toes as though hanging in agony from his outstretched arms. "Oh, you bloodhounds of detectives who do your masters' evil bidding. Oh, you district attorneys." His eyes were flung up to the courtroom ceiling. "You know not what you do."

He had neglected to refute the strong evidence that had been a party to the bribe offer, but the spellbound jury overlooked the omission and acquitted him on the first ballot.

Still, the State of California wasn't through with him. On January 20, 1913, he was brought to trial again for bribing the second juror, Edward Bain. This time Darrow gradually demoted the supposed chief counsel, Earl Rogers, to sitting in silence like a schoolboy being punished and let his other lawyers, including a later-famous assistant named Jerry Geisler, handle the questioning. Clarence Darrow was putting his total trust in another stirring final address to the jury.

His confidence was too obvious. He wasn't the same sympathy-rousing figure he had previously been. To his astonishment, the jury couldn't reach a verdict. His final vote was eight to four for conviction.

California didn't want to try him again. California just wanted to be rid of him. In return for Darrow's written promise that he would never again practice law in the state, he was allowed to catch the next train for Chicago. By that time, he and Rogers hated each other as bitterly as both hated Burns.

None of the three figures in this strange triangle ever

personally crossed paths or swords again, although Earl Rogers won a victory of sorts when Los Angeles finally decided that Burns could not recover its $25,000 reward by reason of having been employed by the city, and gave it instead to Sam Browne. But with this vindictive campaign concluded, Roger's star set rapidly. His extravagances increased, his debts piled up, his bouts with the bottle grew more frequent and prolonged, and his law practice fell apart. He gradually began claiming, in those dazed years of tragic decline, that neither Burns nor Browne but he himself was chiefly responsible for the capture of the dynamiters — a claim he so firmly kept making that his daughter repeated it in a book written fully a half century later. He was only 52 years old when his obituaries were written. He ended as just another dead drunk in a squalid boardinghouse.

Clarence Darrow, by way of contrast, rose above this most embarrassing chapter of his life. He was no longer the nation's leading labor lawyer. Although the men who had emptied work pants pockets for the McNamara fund eventually forgave Samuel Gompers, they had no further use for Darrow. But the Great Defender found other causes in which he lived up to his legend, as when he saved Loeb and Leopold from execution in Chicago, and eloquently argued evolution against William Jennings Bryan in the celebrated Scopes "Monkey" trial. He usually lost his cases, but won moral victories. He was never again accused of jury bribing.

For William J. Burns, the Darrow bribery trials were hardly a turning point for either better or worse, but simply an interruption in some unfinished business. Although the nation in general and the men arguing about the Los Angeles reward in particular seemed to have forgotten the fact, two of the dynamiters were still at large. Month after month and then year after year, Burns kept his pack patiently sniffing out old trails and watching for potential new ones.

He was a busy man those years, making more headlines with new city and state graft investigations, and turning his national detective agency into an international one by opening offices in Montreal, London, Brussels and Paris. He was still a frequent figure of controversy as well. When the Republican Party split into two warring fractions, and the Taft forces were determined to discredit everything connected with Theodore Roosevelt, Burns was a prime target. He had to defend himself against a number of politically motivated charges — including a contention, since repeated by several historians, that the routine juror reports of his men in the land-frauds cases were proof that he had rigged juries for Frank Heney and the President. But as busy as Burns had become, no new operative ever entered his employ without having the photos and habits and histories of David Caplan and Matthew Schmidt drummed into his consciousness.

Finally, in the heart of New York City, some anarchists accidentally blew themselves up with one of their own bombs, leaving behind an explosive device that seemed suspiciously similar to the one Jim McNamara had used. Burns men immediately mounted a surveillance of the neighborhoods and hangouts the dead men had frequented. On February 13, 1915, a beefy, red-faced fellow left a furnished room at Broadway and 66th Street, walked two blocks south and suddenly found himself overpowered and handcuffed. Matthew A. Schmidt was finally in custody.

Weeks of shadowing him had given no hint of his old partner's whereabouts, but some letters found in Schmidt's room were more revealing. Two Burns men boarded a train for Chicago, picked up two more for the trip on to Seattle, enlisted the help of local police, then rented a boat for a nighttime ride across Rolling Bay to Bainbridge Island. There, in an isolated house on the outskirts of an anarchist colony, they surprised David Caplan in bed, subduing him before he could use the revolver he kept under his pillow.

Both he and Schmidt were brought to Los Angeles for trial, where Ortie McManigal, who had been granted immunity in return for his cooperation, had to return to the public spotlight to testify. (McManigal later had a normal career as a county watchman, using the name W. E. Mack and retiring only in 1944.) With no Gompers to raise funds for them and no Darrow to defend them, David Caplan and Matthew Schmidt were quickly convicted and sentenced to life imprisonment.

The biggest chase of the young century was finally over, and its end had been something of a family affair. The Burns operative who had led the cross-country trip to get Caplan, after playing a major part in capturing Schmidt, was a young man whose college career had been bracketed by the long hunt. Sherman Burns had enrolled at Stanford in the weeks between the Peoria explosions and the *Times* building blast. Through all the summers and holidays he had worked for the agency, as well as the eight months that had gone by since graduation, his most fervent ambition had been to be present at the windup his father had never permitted anyone to doubt would be coming — the close of the clientless case that had dominated the Burns Agency for fully four and a half years.

By then, however, all of the rewards except the Los Angeles one had been paid to the agency and distributed as promised to the operatives involved — a total of about $50,000, including $10,000 posted by the State of California. Whatever Earl Rogers' private split of the $25,000 paid by the City of Los Angeles may have been, he hardly profited from his extended involvement in the whole affair. When the Great Defender, Clarence Darrow, had been offered the chance to get out of the state instead of standing trial again, he had neglected to pay the man who had defended him. Rogers went to his grave with the $27,000 Darrow owed him still on his books.

In later years, William J. Burns would insist to reporters

that some aspects of human nature remained a relative constant in a world of accelerating change. "Crooks are still crooks," he'd say, and then wryly add, with a bluntness that never left him: "And lawyers are still lawyers!"

PART SIX

Front-Page Detective

At about 3:30 A. M. on the morning of April 27, 1913, a night watchman named Newt Lee carried a lantern through the coal cellar of a pencil factory in Atlanta, Georgia. The weak circle of light outlined what seemed a bundle of clothes on a pile of ashes in a corner. But when the watchman moved closer, the bundle proved to be the strangled and apparently violated body of a 14-year-old girl named Mary Phagan.

Newt Lee, a Negro, was almost hysterical as he tried to phone the factory superintendent, a 30-year-old man named Leo Frank. There was no answer at the Frank home. Lee then called the police, though he was sickly certain they would arrest him as a matter of course — which they promptly did. But even the police were stunned by the incredible amount of sensational coverage the press gave the crime. A reporter named Harold Ross, covering the case for the Atlanta *Journal,* looked back later on those frantic days and summed up the reaction with superb clarity:

> The murder of Mary Phagan was the most brutal crime in the annals of the South. After the unfolding of the details, the police did what they always do in Georgia — arrested a Negro . . . .
> But this time the public was not satisfied. The furor

did not die down in two or three days, as it had in the cases the police had to deal with in the past. Baffled in their hunt for the real slayer, they at the same time realized something else must be done. So they arrested more Negroes. But this did not stop the clamor.

The crime was an abnormal one; it outshadowed all previous ones. The police realized the truth which determined their whole future course of action:

The murder of Mary Phagan must be paid for with blood. And a Negro's blood would not suffice.

A half-dozen days after the discovery of the body, Leo Frank, who had given the dead girl her wages at noon on April 26 and was the last person to admit seeing her alive, was taken into custody.

There was little that resembled real evidence against him. But Leo Frank was Jewish, and with the ugly public mood taking on anti-Semitic overtones, he was understandably frightened enough to hire a detective as well as a lawyer, retaining a man named Harry Scott from the local Pinkerton office. It proved a tragic choice. Scott was better suited to watching racetrack touts than tackling a major crime. He had never before worked on a murder case, and he disliked Jews. Keeping Frank's trust and confidence, he privately decided that his client was guilty and worked determinedly to build a case against him.

Before long, detective Scott was boasting to newsmen that he had "personally collected enough evidence to convict the murderer of Mary Phagan." The nature of this alleged evidence was never revealed, but within a few weeks it was unneeded. In late May, Scott played a leading role in obtaining what seemed the strongest evidence possible, the testimony of a supposed confederate after the fact.

Among the "more Negroes" arrested by the police just after the murder was a sweeper from the factory named Jim Conley. He sat in jail for nearly a month before anyone bothered questioning him. But once such questioning began, carried on by Pinkerton man Scott and two city detectives, it continued for days. Finally, on May 28, sweeper Jim Conley signed a long statement accusing superintendent Leo Frank of the murder.

According to Conley's story, Frank was a pervert and a lecher who had had frequent trysts with the young girls employed at the factory. On the day of Mary Phagan's death, the sweeper asserted, the superintendent had called him, shown him the limp figure on the floor, and explained that he had struck the girl when she resisted him. Jim Conley further insisted that Frank ordered him to help hide the body in the coal cellar.

In early August, Frank went on trial for murder, with Conley as the state's star witness and angry mobs massing outside the courthouse chanting, "Hang the Jew, or we'll hang you." The courtroom drama dominated the front pages of newspapers the nation over. Detective Harry Scott told reporters that, if his former client were acquitted, the Pinkertone Agency would be "all through in Atlanta." The presiding judge was certain that an acquittal would mean a lynching; he ruled that Frank could not be in court to hear his own verdict. The national guard was alerted and held in readiness.

The public reaction to an acquittal was never learned. The national guard was unneeded at the time. On August 25, Leo Frank was found guilty as charged, and he was soon sentenced to be hung by the neck until dead. Already, a folk song had materialized:

> *Little Mary Phagan*
> *Went to town one day,*
> *Went to the pencil factory*
> *To get her little pay.*
>
> *Leo Frank, he met her*
> *With an evil heart and grin . . . .*

There are several versions of the words, which are still

occasionally sung in rural pockets of the South.

From the beginning, rumors had been circulating that William J. Burns would soon be entering the case. This was not unusual; every sensational murder or mystery of the day brought speculation that he would soon be on the scene, and the part a Pinkerton man had played in this particular case heightened the speculation. Burns' well-known rivalry with the Pinkertons was something of a serial brawl those years.

Even so, not until February 14, 1914 — the day after Leo Frank's appeal for a new trial had been turned down by the Georgia Supreme Court — did Burns accept numerous requests that he look into the Mary Phagan murder. On March 5, clearly caught up with enthusiasm for what seemed a lost cause, he announced that he believed Leo Frank innocent, and that he was in the case to stay.

Burns held the national press spotlight steadily for ten days, made headlines when he arrived in Atlanta on March 16, then made more headlines and thoroughly infuriated the local police three days later by asserting that the case was a simple one and that he was confident of clearing it up within a few weeks at most.

Everywhere he went, reporters seemed to be following. Infuriated by whispers that wealthy New York Jews had paid him a fantastic fee, the public was increasingly hostile. When he and the director of his Atlanta office, Dan Lehon, visited the dead girl's home town of Marietta, a growing group of local men began following them down the street, shouting "Jew lovers." One member of the crowd hit Burns from behind, then ducked back among the others yelling, "Lynch him. Lynch him." The crowd rapidly became a wild, roaring mob of hundreds.

Burns and Lehon ran into the nearby courthouse, took out their pistols and grimly got ready to try to save themselves from the attack that seemed certain to erupt. A Marietta judge named Newton Morris heard of what was happening. Hurrying to the scene, he finally got his crazed townsmen to listen to him. He repeatedly reminded them that lynching a man as famous as William J. Burns would beyond doubt mean federal troops and martial law in Georgia. With Judge Morris holding the mob's attention, Burns and Lehon finally managed to slip off to safety.

The Atlanta police were as hostile as the public. They gave Burns no cooperation and made no files available to him except those he could force open with court orders. Despite the obstacles put in his way, the attention he received as a distrusted outsider which restricted his moves, and the fact that countless leads turned up by others had gone dead in the eleven months since the crime, Burns was blandly asserting, by April 4, that he knew the name of the real murderer. On April 23, he publicly accused the state's star witness, Jim Conley, of killing the Phagan girl himself.

Moreover, he had managed to dig up evidence strong enough to prove this conclusion to the satisfaction of most researchers who have studied the case since.

Burns had found a star witness of his own, a Negro woman named Annie Maude Carter who had served a jail sentence for theft at the same time Conley was being held on suspicion in the Mary Phagan murder. Conley had become infatuated with Annie Carter, and by her account, he boasted to her that he was the person who had killed the 14-year-old girl in the pencil factory.

This was hardly conclusive in itself; crank and perjured testimony, false affidavits and even false confessions were common in a murder case so highly publicized. But Burns also produced as evidence some one hundred love notes to Annie Carter which were undeniably in Conley's handwriting. In those notes, the man who had accused Leo Frank of perversion and murder proved himself both a pervert and a dangerous psychopath.

Burns was stunned by the reaction to his disclosures. Charges that he had been paid by rich Jews to rig evidence were heard everywhere and even broke into print. The Atlanta police tried to have his associate membership in the

International Association of Police Chiefs revoked. Superior Court Judge Benjamin Hill turned down a move to give Frank a new trial and indicted Burns' director Dan Lehon because he had sent Annie Maude Carter out of the state for her own safety.

Judge Hill insisted he could grant another trial only if "errors of law" existed, no matter how strong the newly-uncovered evidence might be. The Georgia Supreme Court upheld him. By February of 1915, the United States Supreme Court was reviewing the case. But the hearing was limited to the question of whether or not Leo Frank's constitutional rights had been violated by the chanting mob that had terrorized his jury, and Burns' evidence was not considered. With Justices Oliver Wendell Holmes and Charles Evan Hughes dissenting, the appeal was denied.

This left Governor John Slaton of Georgia as Leo Frank's last hope, and Slaton did what the courts had refused to do — he examined Burns' findings. On June 21, in an act of political suicide, he commuted Frank's death sentence.

"The Annie Maude Carter notes, which were not before the jury, were powerful evidence in behalf of the defendant," he wrote in his commutation order. "These letters are the most obscene and lecherous I have ever read."

His courageous move was wasted. On July 17, a fellow prisoner attacked Frank while he slept and slit his throat with a butcher knife. But Frank survived and by August 6, he recovered enough to write Dan Lehon in Atlanta and thank him for all that the Burns Agency had done. Just ten days later, however, twenty-five members of a secret vigilante group that called itself the Knights of Mary Phagan entered the Milledgeville Prison Farm. They dragged Frank out with no resistance from the armed prison guards, drove him 175 miles back to Marietta and hung him there. His throat, only partially healed, broke open again and his jugular vein emptied itself when the noose snapped his neck.

Sweeper Jim Conley, who most qualified later historians

203

have said was the real killer, died of old age in 1962. As reporter Harold Ross had clearly seen, and as William J. Burns, in pitting himself against the local mood, had never really understood, the murder of Mary Phagan had to be paid for in blood, and the blood of a Negro "would not suffice" — not in the south of an era when Negroes were lynched for the most minor of offenses.

Two months after the hanging, the Knights of Mary Phagan burned a cross on the top of Stone Mountain near Atlanta. At the same spot some two weeks later, a self-commissioned "Colonel" named William Simmons initiated a group of these same men into a "reincarnated Invisible Empire of the Knights of the Ku-Klux Klan," profitably proclaiming himself Grand Wizard and resurrecting a remnant of Reconstruction Days that would grow steadily for fully a decade.

William J. Burns had become far more than a detective by that year of 1915, more even than the head of a detective agency that was growing at an unprecedented pace. He had become a national watchdog, accepting assignments that produced evidence of widespread corruption in state and local governments.

Back in 1911, through the same months that found some of his operatives keeping watch on the McNamara brothers, others of them, retained by a group of concerned private citizens, had been quietly investigating the Ohio state legislature. As a consequence, eight legislators soon were charged with accepting bribes, and more indictments followed.

A probe of Illinois legislators came next with similar results, and then Burns operatives went to work exposing dishonesty among West Virginia lawmakers and those of a half-dozen other states. When a citizens' committee began working for reform in Atlantic City, a Burns admirer named Woodrow Wilson, then governor of New Jersey, suggested that the detective be secretly hired. Burns went to Atlantic

City and set up a dummy corporation to promote plans for a new concrete boardwalk. He promised a total of $100,000 in kickbacks to members of the city council, and gave each $500 by way of down payment. There was no difficulty identifying the bribe money later; Burns had marked it with tiny pin-pricks, ordinarily invisible, but spelling out GRAFT when held up to a light.

If Canadians were watching the revelations below the border in smug satisfaction, their turn came in early 1913 when Burns announced the results of a three-month undercover investigation of both houses of the Quebec Legislature.

"Legislators come cheaper in Canada," Burns bluntly told *Harper's Weekly.* "Why, minor members could be bribed for $10 here, $50 there."

By 1915, no state legislator or corporation official anywhere could accept a bribe without wondering if the man offering it might be a Burns detective. And William J. Burns was finally enjoying wealth as well as renown. With his headquarters in New York he bought a beautiful home at Scarborough. He entertained famous friends there, political figures like Al Smith, showmen like John Ringling, and mystery writers like Owen Johnson, whose "Detective McKenna" was one of many fictional sleuths for which Burns was the real-life model.

He had an impressive list of clients by then, including financier J. P. Morgan, and his work for Morgan included such vital assignments as safeguarding the manufacture and shipment of munitions to the Allies early in World War I. His running feud with the Pinkertons raged on year after year, and he was forever involved in controversy of one form or another. Someone was always trying to get his license revoked, but no one ever did.

He made speeches and even went on lecture tours. He was also experiencing some of the family pleasures that he had been forced to bypass during his long years on the road. Back in 1912, his older daughter Florence and her mother had spent a winter renewing old friendships in California, and Florence was introduced to Randal Borough, who had drawn courtroom sketches for the San Francisco *Call* in the graft investigation. Within one year the young artist had moved to New York City and was calling at the Burns home regularly. In the fall of 1915, William J. Burns gave away his first daughter in marriage.

A year later, Sherman Burns married Dorothy Abell, a college chum of his younger sister, Kathleen. Not long afterward, Sherman was off for Europe with the U.S. Army. He returned safely two years later, wearing captain's bars.

Kathleen herself became engaged in 1917 to a young man named Cyrus King, then working for his father as a buyer for the King-Blair clothing store in Detroit. Cyrus went through World War I as a pilot in the infant Navy Air Corps, and he promptly married Kathleen upon his return in 1919. But like his father-in-law 40 years earlier, he seemed to have little taste for going back into the clothing business. He joined the Burns Agency for a time, overhauling its bookkeeping system and designing the Burns sign that is used to this day. Then one day he received a call from an old friend from the war named Charlie Merrill, who was starting a stock-brokerage firm destined to enjoy the same success in its field that Burns had achieved in his. Kathleen's husband settled on a career as a Merrill-Lynch broker, heading the Detroit office until his recent retirement.

Both of William J. Burns' girls had married well. And his sons were really running the Agency — making the all-important, day-by-day decisions that kept a world-wide corporation prospering — while he served chiefly as a public image and spokesman. Now in his sixties and with grandchildren to enjoy, he was dropping into partial retirement. But he could never relax for long. Each time a particularly fascinating case came up, he had to be in on it.

Just before Kathleen's wedding in March of 1919, a mentally-unbalanced woman shot at and missed him in New

206

York's Grand Central Station, later claiming both Divine guidance and mistaken identity. Nine days later, a Long Island district attorney asked the Burns Agency's help with a puzzling murder mystery that had police detectives stymied. The Agency's namesake insisted on handling the case himself.

At about 9:30 P. M., on the night of February 27, a 67-year-old physician named Dr. Robert Keane Wilkins, a big, charming man with long sideburns and a full set of whiskers, had stumbled to the door of a glove manufacturer named Max Mayer, his neighbor in the fashionable community of Long Beach. Dr. Wilkins' derby hat was knocked in on the left side, his overcoat was badly torn and stained with blood, and his face was twisted in pain.

"Mr. Mayer, there have been burglars at my house," he groaned. "Mrs. Wilkins is lying in a pool of blood. They knocked me down and took my watch and chain and pocketbook. Please get help."

Mayer had no telephone. He assisted the stricken doctor to a chair, recalling as he did so that his brother-in-law, who lived in the house, had heard a strange sound a minute or two earlier, a sound he had thought was the cry of a dog being hurt. Mayer rushed to the home of another neighbor, a Mrs. Catherine Schubert, to call the police.

A small crowd of neighbors had gathered at the Wilkins home when officers arrived, and most made angry comments to the effect that this was a further example of the sorry kind of police protection they'd been getting. For weeks, Long Beach had been terrorized by a trio of burglars. Numerous homes had been broken into, and several people had seen the three — one of whom wore a gray cap — running off into the night. Nevertheless, the authorities had made no progress in catching the men.

Mrs. Wilkins was indeed lying in a pool of blood, her skull badly fractured. While some of the neighbors tried to help her, she recovered consciousness just long enough to moan, "Don't hurt me." She was dead before she reached a hospital.

A hammer wrapped in bloodstained newspaper was found in the back yard, along with a lead pipe that bore bloody finger smudges. Dr. Wilkins' empty wallet was lying near a newly painted picket fence.

Questioning the grief-stricken doctor at the Mayer home, the officers learned that Wilkins and his wife had spent the day in Manhattan, where they kept a small apartment in a three-story boardinghouse she owned. After riding the Long Island Railroad home, they had been surprised to see a light in the dining room at the rear of their house. Dr. Wilkins had told his wife to wait while he investigated, but she had evidently been afraid to stay alone and had followed him as he circled around to the back yard. There, he explained, he surprised two men sitting at his table and drinking his wine, one wearing a gray cap. And he had heard someone else ransacking his wife's bedroom. He struggled with the men, was knocked unconscious, and recovered to find his wife lying limp and huddled outside. After doing his best to make her comfortable, he had staggered off for help.

The doctor owned two large collie dogs. One had been found hiding in a corner, severely beaten over the head. The other had been wagging its tail, enjoying the excitement. Dr. Wilkins said that the injured collie was enough of a watchdog to attack burglars, while the other was invariably friendly with strangers.

Meanwhile, Mr. Mayer, Mrs. Schubert and a good many other Long Beach residents were angrily suggesting that the police stop pestering the bloodied, heartsick doctor and get busy catching the murdering burglars.

The police did their best through the days that followed, but seemed to be getting nowhere. Automobiles could enter the area only by crossing a bridge where a private watchman was stationed, and the watchman was certain that no car had left during the hour following 9:30 P.M. He had seen no strangers at any time that evening, and none had been seen at the train station. After checking out all possible boat landings, the idea that the burglars might have moved by sea had to be discarded. A foot-by-foot search of the area, including all of the deserted summer homes, also turned up nothing.

The possibility that Dr. Wilkins, recovering at his Manhattan apartment, had himself commited the crime was considered. But his story was vivid, detailed and highly convincing. Furthermore, he had no apparent reason to kill his wife, and very good reason not to — all the wealth and property in the family was hers. Their marriage had been the third for both, and her will left everything to charity. As long as the lady lived, the elderly doctor enjoyed a luxurious retirement. As a widower, he was practically penniless.

The authorities could only keep on looking for the three elusive burglars, while public indignation over the lack of results steadily mounted. The police themselves could shrug the criticism off; they didn't have to face the voters in the fall election. But Nassau County District Attorney Charles A. Weeks did. On March 13, he desperately phoned the Burns Agency.

It was exactly the kind of case to bring William J. Burns onto the scene with all thought of retirement forgotten. Ordering operative Allen Myers to join him, Burns called on Dr. Wilkins. The two men found the doctor about to catch a train for Long Island. He was worried about his two collies, he explained. He was extremely devoted to the dogs, particularly the injured one that had so bravely attacked the burglars, but he couldn't keep them in the city. They were at a boarding kennel, and he wanted to check up on them.

"Do you mind if we go along?" Burns asked. "There may be something the police are overlooking — something that will help us catch those men."

Wilkins welcomed their company, asserting that he was eager to assist in any way he could. Burns questioned him briefly on the train, then made aimless small talk while they visited the collies — one still wagging its tail; the dog that had been hurt still slinking off.

Alone with Myers later, Burns was blunt and decisive. "The doctor's our man."

"Why?" his assistant wondered.

"Why didn't that dog he's so devoted to seem happy to see him, after two weeks with strangers — unless Wilkins struck the dog himself that night to back up his story?"

"But what reason would he have?" Myers countered. "His wife's will left him broke."

Burns didn't know, but he was convinced that he was right. Investigating further, he found paint smears on the handle of the newspaper-wrapped hammer that matched the paint on the Wilkins' picket fence. Dr. Wilkins had claimed the hammer wasn't his, that the burglars must have brought it with them. In addition, for all the eye witness reports of the doctor's torn and bloodstained clothing the night of the murder, he bore no marks of injury, and there was no record that any medical examination had been made.

Back in Manhattan, Burns and Myers began making inquiries around the neighborhood where the Wilkins' boardinghouse was located. They repeatedly heard gossip that the elderly physician's attentions to pretty young tenants were not exactly grandfatherly. The boardinghouse had become something of a theatrical hotel, in fact, because the doctor always seemed to have rooms available for showgirls and models, while turning away male and older female prospects. There was a rumor that the mother of one young would-be actress had moved her daughter out of the place because of the old man's advances.

Even more interesting was a story Burns heard when he talked with the patrolman on the beat, Nicholas C. Cocks. Some time before the murder, Cocks had caught a burglar in a clothing store. The thief had hit Cocks repeatedly with a hammer wrapped in newspaper before he was overpowered.

The policeman had mentioned the incident to Dr. Wilkins, and the doctor had seemed unusually fascinated by the story, asking about it on several occasions and wondering if burglars often carried hammers wrapped in newspaper.

This was hardly the sort of evidence that could bring a conviction in court, but it did seem to justify calling Dr. Wilkins into District Attorney Weeks' office for further questioning. The doctor was completely cooperative. He even knelt on the floor, in repeating his account of that fatal night, to show how he'd bent over his stricken wife; and he cradled a telephone book in his arms to demonstrate the way he'd lifted her head to make her more comfortable. While he was acting out this scene, Burns detectives back in Manhattan were thoroughly searching his apartment.

There they found pages of the same issue of the weekly newspaper that had been used to wrap the death hammer, and an old work coat with stains of the same green paint that had smudged the hammer handle. Most important, they found a typewritten second will — apparently signed by the dead Mrs. Wilkins but with the date added in the doctor's handwriting. In this document, Dr. Robert Keane Wilkins was most decidedly a beneficiary.

This was on March 16. The next morning, just four days after Burns had entered the case that had been stalemated for two weeks, a warrant was issued for the doctor's arrest.

Wilkins, though, had become suspicious and vanished. He had fled to Baltimore, it was later learned — shaving off his whiskers and sideburns to disguise himself. He tried to slip back to see his lawyer and was recognized and arrested at Pennsylvania Station.

Although Wilkins continued to assert his innocence, Burns men were steadily strengthening the case against him, picking up numerous pieces of minor evidence and proving one inconsistency after another in the story he had told the police. A check of his background showed that he had been a patent-medicine quack, never a real physician. And his second wife had also died under extremely suspicious circumstances.

When the trial began in late June, Burns was his usual dynamic self on the witness stand. When the defense lawyer sarcastically demanded to know how much he'd been paid, Burns promptly produced the bill he was submitting, then wondered aloud if lawyers worked for nothing.

This exchange had nothing to do with the charge against the doctor, but the mass of evidence Burns brought forth proved incontrovertible. The jury said guilty. A short time later, Dr. Robert Keane Wilkins avoided being sentenced by hanging himself in his jail cell.

To newspaper readers, and even to acquaintances at such moments, William J. Burns still seemed to be the detective of genius of the dynamiting case, the Hot Tabasco Burns of the graft investigation. In his sixties now, he looked 15 years younger — still quick and precise in his mannerisms, compelling in his geniality, and explosive in his rage.

The brisk redness he had retained was deceptive, though. The fact was, through too many years of ceaseless activity, he had burned himself out. His great days were behind him. And even at his greatest, he had been essentially an individual detective, never really an able corporation head. His sons Raymond and Sherman were doing a far better job at the complex management of an international detective agency than he himself could have done — even though he most emphatically would have died rather than admit it.

The time had clearly come for him to stay home and play with his grandchildren — to announce his retirement and mean it. And he might well have faced this fact, if that year of 1919 hadn't been bringing tantalizing echoes of his most celebrated triumph. A new wave of anarchist terrorism was sweeping the nation. Bombs were being planted beside homes and offices, or were shipped parcel post to prominent citizens. And the detective who had tracked down anarchist bombers

212

of an earlier era found himself watching impatiently from the sidelines.

Other men were carrying on the fight against the terrorists — and bungling it badly. Instead of tracking down and convicting the guilty individuals, United States Attorney General A. Mitchell Palmer launched a series of "Red Raids," indiscriminately arresting thousands of persons and following the arrests with wholesale deportation hearings. William Flynn, a former Secret Service man, headed the Bureau of Investigation, eventually to be renamed the F.B.I. The Bureau's "General Intelligence Division," to which all antisubversive activity was assigned, was commanded by a man just 24 years old — J. Edgar Hoover.

Then, on September 16, 1920, a driverless wagon drawn by a single horse suddenly exploded at noon on Wall Street, directly across from the J. P. Morgan offices. Like a gigantic hand-grenade blast, small pieces of cast iron shot out in all directions. Twenty-nine people were killed immediately. Four died later. And fully three hundred were injured, a third of them seriously.

To William J. Burns, bursting back into action, it seemed the Los Angeles *Times* building case all over again, a chance to relive his finest hour. At that moment of general remorse over the excesses of the Palmer raids, the nation wanted to believe the tragedy was an accident. There were reports that the wagon, loaded with blasting powder and on its way to a nearby excavation, had by mischance gone off.

But Burns regarded this talk of an accident as no more reasonable than allegations that bursting gas mains in Los Angeles a decade earlier were responsible for the *Times'* disaster. The explosion had been much too powerful for mere powder. It blew open a great crater in the pavement and hurled a deadly shower of cast-iron slugs as far as five blocks, frequently over the tops of high buildings. These slugs, some four inches long, were clearly not the result of a

213

large piece of cast iron being shattered; the rust on their smooth rounded edges proved this conclusively. All the evidence suggested a huge device with either dynamite or nitroglycerin at the core of a load of slugs.

There were additional facts to suggest that someone had intentionally sprayed the area with a Bunyanesque shotgun blast. The New York City records required for the shipment of explosives did not show a wagonload of powder or anything else missing. And no explosive was scheduled to be on Wall Street that day. Furthermore, there was fresh grass in the stomach of the scorched and disemboweled horse. This indicated that the animal had come from somewhere out of town, since city horses were generally fed hay. Pieces of the shattered red wagon were collected, and a partial reconstruction made it seem likely that the vehicle had a wider wheelbase than those usually used in New York, which were built narrow to run on the trolly tracks.

Still, there was nothing that could be traced except a set of horseshoes and some sections of a harness. The New York police publicly clung to the accident theory for six days, then finally admitted the blast must have been a bombing; but they made no further progress in investigating it. All over the nation, the Bureau of Investigation was making arrests and repeatedly announcing that a break in the case was close at hand. But one by one, various suspects were cleared. And the Wall Street disaster remained a mystery.

Working independently, William J. Burns eventually found the blacksmith who had fitted the dead horses's shoes, and then the harness maker who had repaired the harness, both upstate at Syracuse. After about six months of investigation, he was even certain he knew the identity of the death-wagon driver, an anarchist from Poland who used a dozen different names. But this suspect had sailed for Europe immediately after the explosion.

Finally, in December of 1921, Burns' agents arrested a man named Wolfe Linderfeld in Warsaw, a radical whom the

Burns Agency had previously attempted to use as an informer only to find him completely unreliable. Linderfeld made a long written statement in which he described the Wall Street bombing plot in great detail. His story contained names and dates and places already known to the investigators. And for a time, Burns was certain the clearing up of the case was close at hand.

But Linderfeld resisted extradition and repudiated his statement. By late 1922, when he was finally brought to the United States, he had changed his story so often the newspapers were dubbing him "Windy Lindy." Burns questioned him briefly at Ellis Island, and realized immediately that the man was merely repeating gossip about the Wall Street bombing he had heard in European anarchist circles. Linderfeld was promptly shipped back to Poland.

For years, the Burns Agency offices in Europe kept up the hunt for the man Burns was certain had driven the bomb wagon. But as successfully as Burns' undercover operatives had once worked in the anarchist shacktowns of the American northwest, the slums of the Old World cities proved far more formidable cover. The fugitive's trail was picked up and lost several times, but he was never found. Burns came to believe he was somewhere in Russia.

The Burns men who had been sent after Linderfeld in late 1921, incidentally, had been Justice Department agents, not his private operatives. For on August 19 of that year, in what hindsight can call the worst mistake of his life, William J. Burns had accepted an appointment as Director of the federal Bureau of Investigation, which newsmen were already dubbing the F.B.I.

President Warren G. Harding had come to office with the fond notion of returning the nation to the "normalcy" of the McKinley era. He announced a policy of gathering the "best minds" in the country about him. He wanted men like Charles Evan Hughes and Andrew Mellon and future-President Herbert Hoover in his cabinet. And he wanted, as head of either the Bureau of Investigation, or the Secret Service, or possibly both under a reorganization plan he had been pondering, "the only detective of genius the country had produced" — William J. Burns.

Harding got Hughes and Mellon and Hoover to join his cabinet. He was far less fortunate in several of his other selections, including the choice of his campaign manager, Harry Daugherty, as Attorney General.

All through early 1921, newspapers carried conflicting reports as to whether Burns would replace Secret Service Chief W. Herman Moran or Bureau of Investigation Director William Flynn. Moran waited in silence and hoped for the best. Flynn, beyond doubt regretting the fact that he had often told reporters Burns was the greatest detective he'd ever met, campaigned frantically to have Congressmen and judges write to President Harding and urge that he be retained. And A.F. of L. President Samuel Gompers, still smarting from the humiliation he had endured a decade earlier, announced that organized labor was opposed to Burns' receiving either post.

Largely at the urging of Attorney General Daugherty, who had met Burns around the turn of the century and remained something of a casual social acquaintance, Burns accepted command of the Bureau of Investigation.

While Burns accepted the post partly because of a desire to return to the national limelight, there were at least two important things he felt he could accomplish as Bureau Director. On the record, he did both.

Burns believed that fingerprinting was a far more effective method of identifying criminals than the Bertillon system of using a long list of physical characteristics. Just one month after taking office, he announced he would set up a National Bureau of Identification, and he immediately began gathering copies of fingerprints from various police departments that were already using them. A good many Congressmen were hostile to Burns; he had stepped on numerous toes through the years, particularly during his series of graft investigations of state legislatures. As a result, the money needed to make use of fingerprints was never appropriated during his term as Director. But the files were ready and waiting when funds were forthcoming.

Burns also believed that the Ku-Klux Klan was a sinister threat no longer confined to the South; he remembered very vividly the Marietta mob that had attempted to lynch Dan Lehon and himself, had gone on to hang Leo Frank, and then became the nucleus of the reincarnated Klan. Just two months after taking office, he was testifying at length and in strong terms before Congress and making it clear that he intended to force a showdown with the white-sheeted brotherhood.

His chance came in September of 1922, when Governor John M. Parker of Louisiana asked Burns for help, sending a letter in the care of a trusted newspaperman because the Klan was opening his mail and tapping his telephone. Parker claimed that the Klan ruled northern Louisiana, beating, abducting, and even murdering its opposition. The governor insisted that he was helpless because "law officers and others charged with the enforcement of law in this State are publicly recognized as members of the Ku-Klux Klan."

This plea provided the legal authorization needed, and Burns promptly dispatched special squads of federal agents to seek out and work with law officers and prosecutors who were not Klan members or sympathizers. Convictions were rare at first. Even so, Klan lawlessness now was exposed regularly, stripping the secret society of any pretense of respectability. The most vital victory came when Bureau of Investigation men arrested Imperial Kleagle Edward Clarke at New Orleans and secured indictments in Texas against him on white slavery charges, to which he subsequently pleaded guilty.

As late as 1925, the Ku-Klux Klan was able to muster 50,000 marchers for a demonstration in Washington, D.C. But this show of strength was deceptive, a last defiant gasp from an organization that was already disintegrating rapidly under the relentless federal attack. The Klan would decline to impotency within a very few years. Never again — even when the Supreme Court's school-integration ruling offered the same kind of racist pretext for reincarnation that opportunists had once seen in the murder of Mary Phagan — did the Klan attain the power it had known in the early 1920's.

The victory over the KKK was all the more impressive in light of the fact that the Bureau of Investigation that Burns headed was by no means the politically-free organization of professionals that exists today. Appointments of agents were commonly made by the Attorney General as favors, and the Director was informed after the fact. Moreover the Attorney General, the President, and even the President's wife on occasion, felt perfectly free to borrow Bureau men for confidential missions about which Burns was told nothing.

Burns did have one competent aid. Young J. Edgar Hoover, already demonstrating the remarkable staying power that would soon become legendary, had not only survived the change in administration that had cost Palmer and Flynn their jobs, but had been promoted to Assistant Director. But Burns had numerous bad appointments forced upon him, and he admittedly made some blunders of his own — the worst of which was his use of a curious character named Gaston Means.

Means was a type of uninhibited scoundrel that all successful investigatory organizations enlist from time to time. Although raised in North Carolina, he had been a German secret agent in 1916 when Burns first heard of him. At the time, Burns was on retainer from the Morgan firm to keep munitions secrets from German intelligence. Contacting Means, he had "doubled" the man — paying him to inform on his employers.

Means had severed his German connections when the United States entered World War I — less from patriotism that from difficulty in getting paid — and had taken up with a wealthy widow named Maude King. When she passed away suddenly and mysteriously, he was charged with her murder.

But he had been acquitted, although the evidence was reasonably clear that he had bilked her out of at least $150,000.

Means had proved of value before, and Burns had need of a rogue or two in the Bureau of Investigation. But he soon discovered to his dismay that rogues were far more at home in the Washington of that era than he was. Gaston Means got out of his control by ingratiating himself with Attorney General Daugherty, and was soon carrying out furtive assignments for the cabinet member. Before long, if his own account can be believed, Means was privately investigating Warren G. Harding's affairs of heart and paternity for Mrs. Harding, and even indulging in what might be called blackmail of the President of the United States.

However factual Means' later accounts may be, the record is clear that, within a few months, this man whom Burns had originally doubled as a German agent had been redoubled more than a few times and had lost his usefulness to Burns and finally to Daugherty as well. With his customary knack for coming out of a bad situation, Means wangled a job as a prohibition agent.

Obviously, the Washington in which William J. Burns now found himself was a far cry from the Washington where he had moved so surefootedly twenty years earlier. There was no Ethan Allen Hitchcock standing like a granite wall behind him. Instead, there was Harry Daugherty, unabashedly playing politics with every move he made. There was no Teddy Roosevelt to tell Burns to root out the rascals no matter how highly placed they might be. There was only Warren G. Harding, far beyond his depth in the Presidency, perhaps wielding less power in the White House than his own wife did.

Furthermore, Burns simply wasn't the same gifted graft detector he had been in the days when he cleaned out the General Land Office from top to bottom. Charles Forbes, a close friend of President Harding, was plundering the Veteran's Bureau; another White House intimate named Tom Miller was growing rich on kickbacks from Alien Property Claims, and Secretary of the Interior Albert Fall was selling the Teapot Dome and Elk Hills government oil preserves to the highest bribers. But like a bloodhound past its prime, Burns' nose for corruption had left him.

It may be unfair to say that Burns — or his assistant J. Edgar Hoover, for that matter — should have seen and exposed the scandal being spawned in the Harding Administration. Secretary of Commerce Herbert Hoover was far closer to Fall, Miller and Forbes, and yet he had no hint of what was going on. Even today, with the F.B.I. kept antiseptically free of political influence, no one expects its director to keep the President's close friends under surveillance or have cabinet members shadowed. Burns' immediate superior was the Attorney General, and although no charge was ever proven against him, most historians believe Daugherty himself was in on the chicanery.

But even so, it can safely be said that had the William J. Burns of a decade or two earlier been commanding the Bureau of Investigation, the 1920's would have been another chronicle entirely.

Warren G. Harding died in office in mid-1923. Calvin Coolidge became President, but made few changes in government, in spite of scathing and increasing criticism from Congress. Early 1924 found Attorney General Daugherty, the main target of Congressional critics, locked in a bitter dispute with Senator Burton K. Wheeler of Montana. On February 20, Wheeler delivered a vehement attack on the Attorney General.

Publicly, Daugherty responded by calling the Senator a radical. Privately, Daugherty told Burns that Wheeler was creating a smokescreen to cover up the fact that he was using his office to get lucrative federal oil leases for private clients. Burns dispatched three agents to Montana to get the facts.

The facts were these: Senator Wheeler had received $10,000 as a retainer for representing a wealthy oil man named Gordon Campbell — but in the courts of Montana, not federal courts. The only thing the Senator had done that might be called questionable was to contact the Department of the Interior and make an appointment for Campbell.

This was hardly clear evidence of conflict of interest, and Burns expected to hear no more of the matter. But suddenly and unexpectedly, Senator Wheeler's campaign against Daugherty got a strong assist — from the forgotten Gaston Means.

Means had been indicted for a scheme in which he swindled some bootleggers by telling them he was collecting graft for the Secretary of the Treasury. Blaming his old friend Harry Daugherty for not squelching the charges against him, Means offered himself to Senator Wheeler as a star witness against the Attorney General.

No one will ever know how much of Means' testimony was true. (He went to prison and upon his release wrote a best-selling book in which he claimed, among other things, that Mrs. Harding had poisoned the late President; then Means went back to prison for a swindle connected with the Lindbergh kidnapping.) But he had a highly sympathetic audience in 1924 when he charged that Harry Daugherty, without the knowledge of Burns or J. Edgar Hoover, had hired him to employ teams of private detectives to compile secret files on numerous Senators. Means' accusations brought on a storm of outrage that President Coolidge couldn't ignore. On March 24, he asked for the Attorney General's resignation.

Just eleven days later, in what patently appeared to be retaliation, a federal grand jury in Montana indicted Senator Wheeler, charging he had used his office to get oil leases for Gordon Campbell.

Burns was puzzled. He knew his men had turned up nothing resembling a case against Wheeler. He was even more puzzled when Daugherty told newsmen that the Justice Department had absolutely nothing to do with Wheeler's indictment, that the charge was solely the action of a U.S. District Attorney in Montana.

Burns had to face the truth then: not only was Daugherty

lying; the former Attorney General was obviously expecting the prestigious Director of the Bureau of Investigation to back up his story.

No one will ever know what William J. Burns was thinking when he went before the United States Senate on April 24, 1924. Described as "ashen-faced" by *The New York Times* , he may have been inwardly staring back in an attempt to see some semblance of meaning or purpose in all the shifting political crosscurrents through which he had plied his trade. Right-wing Republicans had attacked him for exposing the land frauds. Unions had vilified him for putting Abe Ruef in prison. The wealthy interests of the West had assaulted him again for going after Patrick Calhoun and United Railroads. And the nation's leading labor officials had never forgiven him for the fact that the McNamaras were guilty. Burns may have been contemplating all of this and then shrugging it off — finally seeing himself, for all his prominence, as essentially in pawn to larger patterns of social change, as buffeted about by a nation's growing pains.

On the other hand, he may merely have been wishing he had stayed home and played with his grandchildren.

Whatever the case, he told the Senate the simple truth — contradicting his former boss and friend Daugherty by giving a full account of the three agents he had sent to Montana and telling exactly what they reported. He answered all questions readily but tonelessly. And little more than two weeks later, he resigned as Director of the Bureau of Investigation.

He and Annie had a winter home at Sarasota, Florida, and they made it a permanent residence as he tried to relax at last. But it was really too late. Burns' blood pressure was bad, his digestion was troubling him, and even in full retirement, controversy wouldn't leave him alone.

In 1927, an oil man named Harry Sinclair, one of the accused bribers of Secretary of the Interior Albert Fall, asked the Burns Agency to keep his jurors under surveillance to make sure they weren't being tampered with — a reasonable request to make in light of the Washington mood that prevailed at the height of the Teapot Dome scandal. The Agency accepted the assignment, and Sinclair was acquitted. However, the federal judge who tried the case was furious. He ruled that jury shadowing was itself a form of jury tampering, and fined the Burns Agency $1,000. William J. Burns, now 69, burst back onto the front pages again.

"My men didn't do anything for Harry Sinclair that I haven't done for the federal government hundreds of times!" he exploded, and he added a few harsh comments in his rage that left him charged with contempt of court. He was sentenced to fifteen days in jail, but he never served the sentence. His case was appealed, and the contempt citation was eventually thrown out.

A stormy public figure to the very end, William J. Burns died in April of 1932, his heart failing after several spells of serious illness.

Annie Ressler Burns lived on until 1958, long enough to see a third generation assume active leadership in the corporation her husband had created — grandsons D. Bruce Burns, William J. Burns III, George Edward Burns King, grandson-in-law John D. O'Connor. A great-granddaughter with a French governess began calling her *grandmere,* and she was soon *grandmere* to all. She had come a long, strange way for a sensible girl who married a tailor's son in Columbus, Ohio. Calmly and competently, she had accepted whatever the world brought her, from carrying in her own coal to entertaining presidents. In her last years, as the fountainhead of a rare family closeness, she was, in a sense, the matriarch of the world's largest detective agency.

To all too many today, her husband is little more than the name of a corporation or the wording on a warning sign. The incredible roll call of cases he personally solved grew hazy as new crimes captured the public imagination. The

Harding era clouded his last years and left him libeled or ignored in the history books.

Yet the total record suggests he was exactly what *The New York Times* called him — "the greatest detective certainly, and perhaps the only really great detective, the only detective of genius whom the country has produced." And he deserves to be remembered as such. For the country that produced him was a different America — younger, simpler, more flamboyant and yet somehow more innocent in both its vices and virtues — and there will never be another like him.